Virtual Philosophy

Adventures in
Digital Reality

David Christopher Lane, Kelly Diem-Lane

Mt. San Antonio College
Walnut, California

Virtual Philosophy

Format Copyright © 2022 MSAC Philosophy Group

First Edition | Trade paperback

ISBN: 978-1-56543-958-0

General Editors: Dr. Andrea Diem and Dr. David Lane

MSAC Philosophy Group was founded in 1990 and is designed to provide a wide range of materials (from books to magazines to films to audio presentations to interactive texts) on such subjects as evolutionary biology, quantum theory, neuroscience, and critical studies in religion and philosophy. All books are sold on a not for profit basis. Free PDF versions are made available whenever possible. In addition, there is a growing collection of audio books specifically created for students at Mt. San Antonio College and the community at large. A large series of original movies have also been produced which touch on such topics as artificial intelligence, eliminative materialism, consciousness, and skepticism.

When children are growing up, they face a profound conflict between the internal world of their dreams and imagination, in which everything's possible and fluid, and the practical world in which they have parents, food, and friends, in which they're not alone, and in which they can survive. So as kids grow up, they have to gradually de-emphasize this world of imagination and celebration and emphasize the practical world, unless they're willing to be alone in their insanity and completely dependent on others for survival. Of course it's possible to integrate the two, but it's so hard, like walking a tightrope. I think the reason that kids instinctively love computers, and especially love virtual reality, is that it really does present a new solution, a way to make imaginary worlds that we can be together in, just like the real world.

--Jaron Lanier

Table of Contents

Introduction

I have always wanted to teach a philosophy course utilizing virtual reality technologies. I first introduced the Oculus Quest headset just prior to the onset of the Covid 19 epidemic and it was a huge hit with my students. However, because of the lockdown and mask requirements, we were unfortunately delayed in offering a class that fully integrated VR. Now, thankfully, the time has arrived that makes it possible to incorporate the full potential of virtual reality into the classroom.

The following workbook contains twelve distinct assignments that are based on various virtual reality applications and games currently available on the Oculus Quest 2 headset (now rebranded as Meta). Each module focuses on a different aspect of philosophical inquiry, ranging from existentialism to idealism to political science to consciousness studies to the latest developments in artificial intelligence, etc.

The structure of each assignment is as follows: 1. Instruction. 2. Reading. 3. VR engagement. 4. Completion. While several of the modules include writing essays, usually in an autobiographical or experimental format, many are concerned with creating new and distinctive content within virtual reality. This includes composing a short soundtrack to accompany a particularly ponderous and deep insight, constructing a new version of Plato's famous "Allegory of the Cave," and building a unique city from the ground up to better understand the necessary checks and balances necessary to manage a thriving and industrious community.

This workbook is just one of three required for the "Virtual Reality Philosophy Course" being offered here at Mt. San Antonio College. The second one is entitled, *Digital Teleportation: A Philosophic Journey in Virtuality,* which at over three hundred pages long contains twenty-five original articles on neuroscience, machine learning, evolutionary biology, and the future of virtual, augmented, and mixed reality. The third required text, and the guiding philosophical overview for the class, is David Chalmers' book, *Reality+: Virtual Worlds and the Problems of Philosophy.*

Each student will also be required to create their own website which will house all the work—written or otherwise—that they produce during the course of the semester and which they can share with their fellow cohorts to exchange ideas.

One may ask why it is necessary to have VR technologies in the classroom, since most traditional philosophy courses follow a Socratic method of inquiry and tend to rely on written tests exclusively. The answer is that VR doesn't do away with classic methods of pedagogy but rather opens up new ways to explore age-old philosophical questions, especially in light of the latest scientific advances in deep learning.

Instead of merely reading about Pythagoras' notion concerning the "music of the spheres" you journey into the heart of the cosmos, listening and seeing and feeling what it is like to be enveloped into a black hole or plunging head first into the inner core of our sun. VR literally changes how we interact with information and in the process we can embody what before was only the province of imagination.

I have no doubt that the future of schooling will be radically transformed by the coupling of artificial intelligence and virtual reality technologies. It has already started to happen and this interactive course at Mt. San Antonio College is a pioneering attempt to open new vistas on how we access knowledge. Preparing students for what the future has in store for them is of vital importance. Being able to think "wisely" in an age of ever-increasing technological complexity is precisely what Aristotle would have advised if he lived and taught today.

Virtual Philosophy

Professor Lane's Course Using VR Technology

ASSIGNMENT MODULE ONE | ORIGINAL MUSICAL SCORE

VIRTUOSO APPLICATION

INSTRUCTIONS: After closely reading the following essays, create a piece of original music that can accompany only one of the chosen texts and brings out the proper mood of what the author was trying to convey. Do this by using the Virtuoso application on your VR headset. There is a learning curve, but you don't need any prior training in music to create a unique song. The piece that you create should be only 3 to 4 minutes in length, correlated to the length of the article. When finished be sure to export it and download it so it can be accessed on a computer. Place the file on your own website and also share it with your chosen cohorts and the larger class. After this then sync your music with the text and then create a visual-auditory on YouTube film by placing the text accompanied by the music you created. This you can do using any movie-making program. Place the link to your YouTube video on your website and also share it with your chosen cohorts and the larger class. Make sure all that you post is publicly accessible.

Choose Only One To Create a Sound Track

NIETZSCHE'S THE MADMAN AND THE "DEATH" OF GOD

THE MADMAN----Have you not heard of that madman who lit a lantern in the bright morning hours, ran to the market place, and cried incessantly: "I seek God! I seek God!"---As many of those who did not believe in God were standing around just then, he provoked much laughter. Has he got lost? asked one. Did he lose his way like a child? asked another. Or is he hiding? Is he afraid of us? Has he gone on a voyage? emigrated?---Thus they yelled and laughed

The madman jumped into their midst and pierced them with his eyes. "Whither is God?" he cried; "I will tell you. *We have killed him*---you and I. All of us are his murderers. But how did we do this? How could we drink up the sea? Who gave us the sponge to wipe away the entire horizon? What were we doing when we unchained this earth from its sun? Whither is it moving now? Whither are we moving? Away from all suns? Are we not plunging continually? Backward, sideward, forward, in all directions? Is there still any up or down? Are we not straying, as through an infinite nothing? Do we not feel the breath of empty space? Has it not become colder? Is not night continually closing in on us? Do we not need to light lanterns in the morning? Do we hear nothing as yet of the noise of the gravediggers who are burying God? Do we smell nothing as yet of the divine decomposition? Gods, too, decompose. God is dead. God remains dead. And we have killed him.

"How shall we comfort ourselves, the murderers of all murderers? What was holiest and mightiest of all that the world has yet owned has bled to death under our knives: who will wipe this blood off us? What water is there for us to clean ourselves? What festivals of atonement, what sacred games shall we have to invent? Is not the greatness of this deed too great for us? Must we ourselves not become gods simply to appear worthy of it? There has never been a greater deed; and whoever is born after us---for the sake of this deed he will belong to a higher history than all history hitherto."

Here the madman fell silent and looked again at his listeners; and they, too, were silent and stared at him in astonishment. At last he threw his lantern on the ground, and it broke into pieces and went out. "I have come too early," he said then; "my time is not yet. This tremendous event is still on its way, still wandering; it has not yet reached the ears of men. Lightning and thunder require time; the light of the stars requires time; deeds, though done, still require time to be seen and heard. This deed is still more distant from them than most distant stars---*and yet they have done it themselves.*

It has been related further that on the same day the madman forced his way into several churches and there struck up his *requiem aeternam deo*. Led out and called to account, he is said always to have replied nothing but: "What after all are these churches now if they are not the tombs and sepulchers of God?"

Source: *Friedrich Nietzsche, The Gay Science (1882, 1887) para. 125; Walter Kaufmann ed. (New York: Vintage, 1974), pp.181-82.]*

Excerpts from Søren Kierkegaard's Repetition

ON THE IMPOSSIBILITY OF CONTENTMENT

BY M.G. PIETY

Is it not the case that the older one becomes the more life reveals itself to be deceptive, the smarter one becomes, the more ways one learns to help himself, the worse off he is, the more one suffers. A small child is completely helpless and yet thrives. I remember once having seen a nursemaid on the street pushing a baby carriage in which there were two children. The one, just barely a year old, had fallen asleep and lay in the carriage dead to the world. The other was a little girl around two years old, chubby in short sleeves just like a little woman. She had pushed herself forward in the carriage and easily took up two thirds of the space. The smaller child lay next to her as if it were a package the woman had brought with her. With an admirable egoism, she appeared not to care for anyone or anything except herself, if she could just make herself comfortable. Then a coach came down the road. The baby carriage was clearly in danger. People ran to help, but with one healthy shove, the nurse managed to push the carriage into a doorway. Everyone was horrified, including myself. Yet throughout this commotion, the little Madame was completely calm. She continued peacefully to pick her nose, her expression never changing. Presumably she thought, what do I care? It is the nurse's problem. One will seek in vain for such courageousness in an older person.

The older one gets, the better he understands life and the more he comes to care for and appreciate comfort. In short, the more competent one becomes, the less content. One will never be completely, absolutely and in every way content, and it is hardly worth the trouble to be more or less content, so one might as well be thoroughly discontented. Anyone who has really thought through the issue, will agree with me that no one is ever granted even as little as a half an hour out of his entire life where he is absolutely content in every conceivable way. It goes without saying that more is required for this sort of contentment than that one has food and clothing. I was close to achieving it once. I got up one morning in unusually good humor. This positive mood actually expanded, as the morning progressed, in a manner I had never before experienced. By one o'clock, my mood had climaxed and I sensed the dizzying heights of complete contentment, a level that appears on no scale designed to measure moods, not even on the poetic thermometer. My body no longer seemed weighed down by gravity. It was as if I had no body in that every function hummed along perfectly, every nerve rejoiced, the harmony disrupted by each beat of my pulse which served in turn only to remind me of the delightfulness of the moment. I almost floated as I walked, not like the bird, that cuts through the air as it leaves the earth, but like the wind over the fields, like the nostalgic rocking of waves, like the dreamy progress of clouds across the sky. My being was as transparent as the clear depths of the ocean, as the night's self-satisfied stillness, as the soft soliloquy of midday. Every mood resonated melodically in my soul. Every thought, from the most foolish to the most profound, offered itself and offered itself with the same blissful festiveness. Every impression was anticipated before it came and thus awoke from within me. It was as if all of existence were in love with me. Everything quivered in deep rapport with my being. Everything in me was portentous; all mysteries explained in my microcosmic bliss that transfigured everything, even the unpleasant, the most annoying remark, the most loathsome sight, the most fatal collision. As I said, it was exactly at one o'clock that my mood reached its peak, where I sensed the heights of perfect contentment. But then suddenly I got something in my eye. I do not know whether it was an eyelash an insect or a piece of dust. I know this though, that my mood immediately plummeted almost into the abyss of despair. This is something that everyone who has ever experienced these heights of contentment and still speculated to what extent complete contentment was possible, will easily understand. Since that time I have given up any hope of ever being completely contented in every way, given up that hope that I had once nourished, of being, if not always completely content, then at least occasionally completely content even if these occasions never became more numerous than, as Shakespeare put it, "a tapster's [barkeeper's] arithmetic was capable of summing up."

Source: https://www.thesmartset.com/article11020904/

VR NOTES 1

Virtual Philosophy

Professor Lane's Course Using VR Technology

ASSIGNMENT MODULE TWO | ORIGINAL PAINTING

TILT BRUSH APPLICATION

INSTRUCTIONS: After closely reading the following essay, create a piece of original ART that can accompany the text and brings out the proper mood of what the author (Plato via the mouthpiece of Socrates) was trying to convey. Do this by using the Tilt Brush application on your VR headset. There is a learning curve, but you don't need any prior training in ART to create a unique painting or 3D landscape. Be as creative as you wish to be, but the key is that your ART piece should reflect to some degree the content and/or the environment that is inherent in the essay from Plato's *Republic*. Experiment and you can do more than one ART presentation. After you have finished your piece, export it and place it on your website and/or a direct link to it that others can then enjoy. If it is interactive, then make sure to capture it via video and export it as such.

PLATO: THE ALLEGORY OF THE CAVE
from *The Republic*

The son of a wealthy and noble family, Plato (427-347 B.C.) was preparing for a career in politics when the trial and eventual execution of Socrates (399 B.C.) changed the course of his life. He abandoned his political career and turned to philosophy, opening a school on the outskirts of Athens dedicated to the Socratic search for wisdom.

Plato's school, then known as the Academy, was the first university in western history and operated from 387 B.C. until A.D. 529, when it was closed by Justinian.

Unlike his mentor Socrates, Plato was both a writer and a teacher. His writings are in the form of dialogues, with Socrates as the principal speaker. In the Allegory of the Cave, Plato described symbolically the predicament in which mankind finds itself and proposes a way of salvation. The Allegory presents, in brief form, most of Plato's major philosophical assumptions: his belief that the world revealed by our senses is not the real world but only a poor copy of it, and that the real world can only be apprehended intellectually; his idea that knowledge cannot be transferred from teacher to student, but rather that education consists in directing student's minds toward what is real and important and allowing them to apprehend it for themselves; his faith that the universe ultimately is good; his conviction that enlightened individuals have an obligation to the rest of society, and that a good society must be one in which the truly wise (the Philosopher-King) are the rulers.

The Allegory of the Cave can be found in Book VII of Plato's best-known work, The Republic, a lengthy dialogue on the nature of justice. Often regarded as a utopian blueprint, The Republic is dedicated to a discussion of the education required of a Philosopher-King.

The following selection is taken from the Benjamin Jowett translation (Vintage, 1991), pp. 253-261.

[**Socrates**] And now, I said, let me show in a figure how far our nature is enlightened or unenlightened: --Behold! human beings living in a underground cave, which has a mouth open towards the light and reaching all along the cave; here they have been from their childhood, and have their legs and necks chained so that they cannot move, and can only see before them, being prevented by the chains from turning round their heads. Above and behind them a fire is blazing at a distance, and between the fire and the prisoners there is a raised way; and you will see, if you look, a low wall built along the way, like the screen which marionette players have in front of them, over which they show the puppets.

[**Glaucon**] I see.

[**Socrates**] And do you see, I said, men passing along the wall carrying all sorts of vessels, and statues and figures of animals made of wood and stone and various materials, which appear over the wall? Some of them are talking, others silent.

[**Glaucon**] You have shown me a strange image, and they are strange prisoners.

[**Socrates**] Like ourselves, I replied; and they see only their own shadows, or the shadows of one another, which the fire throws on the opposite wall of the cave?

[**Glaucon**] True, he said; how could they see anything but the shadows if they were never allowed to move their heads?

[**Socrates**] And of the objects which are being carried in like manner they would only see the shadows?

[**Glaucon**] Yes, he said.

[**Socrates**] And if they were able to converse with one another, would they not suppose that they were naming what was actually before them?

[**Glaucon**] Very true.

[**Socrates**] And suppose further that the prison had an echo which came from the other side, would they not be sure to fancy when one of the passers-by spoke that the voice which they heard came from the passing shadow?

[**Glaucon**] No question, he replied.

[**Socrates**] To them, I said, the truth would be literally nothing but the shadows of the images.

[**Glaucon**] That is certain.

[**Socrates**] And now look again, and see what will naturally follow if the prisoners are released and disabused of their error. At first, when any of them is liberated and compelled suddenly to stand up and turn his neck round and walk and look towards the light, he will suffer sharp pains; the glare will distress him, and he will be unable to see the realities of which in his former state he had seen the shadows; and then conceive some one saying to him, that what he saw before was an illusion, but that now, when he is approaching nearer to being and his eye is turned towards more real existence, he has a clearer vision, -what will be his reply? And you may further imagine that his instructor is pointing to the objects as they pass and requiring him to name them, - will he not be perplexed? Will he not fancy that the shadows which he formerly saw are truer than the objects which are now shown to him?

[**Glaucon**] Far truer.

[**Socrates**] And if he is compelled to look straight at the light, will he not have a pain in his eyes which will make him turn away to take and take in the objects of vision which he can see, and which he will conceive to be in reality clearer than the things which are now being shown to him?

[**Glaucon**] True, he now.

[**Socrates**] And suppose once more, that he is reluctantly dragged up a steep and rugged ascent, and held fast until he's forced into the presence of the sun himself, is he not likely to be pained and irritated? When he approaches the light his eyes will be dazzled, and he will not be able to see anything at all of what are now called realities.

[**Glaucon**] Not all in a moment, he said.

[**Socrates**] He will require to grow accustomed to the sight of the upper world. And first he will see the shadows best, next the reflections of men and other objects in the water, and then the objects themselves; then he will gaze upon the light of the moon and the stars and the spangled heaven; and he will see the sky and the stars by night better than the sun or the light of the sun by day?

[**Glaucon**] Certainly.

[**Socrates**] Last of he will be able to see the sun, and not mere reflections of him in the water, but he will see him in his own proper place, and not in another; and he will contemplate him as he is.

[**Glaucon**] Certainly.

[**Socrates**] He will then proceed to argue that this is he who gives the season and the years, and is the guardian of all that is in the visible world, and in a certain way the cause of all things which he and his fellows have been accustomed to behold?

[**Glaucon**] Clearly, he said, he would first see the sun and then reason about him. [**Socrates**] And when he remembered his old habitation, and the wisdom of the cave and his fellow-prisoners, do you not suppose that he would felicitate himself on the change, and pity them?

[**Glaucon**] Certainly, he would.

[**Socrates**] And if they were in the habit of conferring honors among themselves on those who were quickest to observe the passing shadows and to remark which of them went before, and which followed after, and which were together; and who were therefore best able to draw conclusions as to the future, do you think that he would care for such honors and glories, or envy the possessors of them? Would he not say with Homer, *Better to be the poor servant of a poor master,* and to endure anything, rather than think as they do and live after their manner?

[**Glaucon**] Yes, he said, I think that he would rather suffer anything than entertain these false notions and live in this miserable manner.

[**Socrates**] Imagine once more, I said, such an one coming suddenly out of the sun to be replaced in his old situation; would he not be certain to have his eyes full of darkness?

[**Glaucon**] To be sure, he said.

[**Socrates**] And if there were a contest, and he had to compete in measuring the shadows with the prisoners who had never moved out of the cave, while his sight was still weak, and before his eyes had become steady (and the time which would be needed to acquire this new habit of sight might be very considerable) would he not be ridiculous? Men would say of him that up he went and down he came without his eyes; and that it was better not even to think of ascending; and if any one tried to loose another and lead him up to the light, let them only catch the offender, and they would put him to death.

[**Glaucon**] No question, he said.

[**Socrates**] This entire allegory, I said, you may now append, dear Glaucon, to the previous argument; the prison-house is the world of sight, the light of the fire is the sun, and you will not misapprehend me if you interpret the journey upwards to be the ascent of the soul into the intellectual world according to my poor belief, which, at your desire, I have expressed whether rightly or wrongly God knows. But, whether true or false, my opinion is that in the world of knowledge the idea of good appears last of all, and is seen only with an effort; and, when seen, is also inferred to be the universal author of all things beautiful and right, parent of light and of the lord of light in this visible world, and the immediate source of reason and truth in the intellectual; and that this is the power upon which he who would act rationally, either in public or private life must have his eye fixed.

[**Glaucon**] I agree, he said, as far as I am able to understand you.

[**Socrates**] Moreover, I said, you must not wonder that those who attain to this beatific vision are unwilling to descend to human affairs; for their souls are ever hastening into the upper world where they desire to dwell; which desire of theirs is very natural, if our allegory may be trusted.

[**Glaucon**] Yes, very natural.

[**Socrates**] And is there anything surprising in one who passes from divine contemplations to the evil state of man, misbehaving himself in a ridiculous manner; if, while his eyes are blinking and before he has become accustomed to the surrounding darkness, he is compelled to fight in courts of law, or in other places, about the images or the shadows of images of justice, and is endeavoring to meet the conceptions of those who have never yet seen absolute justice?

[**Glaucon**] Anything but surprising, he replied.

[**Socrates**] Anyone who has common sense will remember that the bewilderments of the eyes are of two kinds, and arise from two causes, either from coming out of the light or from going into the light, which is true of the mind's eye, quite as much as of the bodily eye; and he who remembers this when he sees any one whose vision is perplexed and weak, will not be too ready to laugh; he will first ask whether that soul of man has come out of the brighter light, and is unable to see because unaccustomed to the dark, or having turned from darkness to the day is dazzled by excess of light. And he will count the one happy in his condition and state of being, and he will pity the other; or, if he have a mind to laugh at the soul which comes from below into the light, there will be more reason in this than in the laugh which greets him who returns from above out of the light into the cave.

[**Glaucon**] That, he said, is a very just distinction.

[**Socrates**] But then, if I am right, certain professors of education must be wrong when they say that they can put a knowledge into the soul which was not there before, like sight into blind eyes.

[**Glaucon**] They undoubtedly say this, he replied.

[**Socrates**] Whereas, our argument shows that the power and capacity of learning exists in the soul already; and that just as the eye was unable to turn from darkness to light without the whole body, so too the instrument of knowledge can only by the movement of the whole soul be turned from the world of becoming into that of being, and learn by degrees to endure the sight of being, and of the brightest and best of being, or in other words, of the good.

[**Glaucon**] Very true.

[**Socrates**] And must there not be some art which will effect conversion in the easiest and quickest manner; not implanting the faculty of sight, for that exists already, but has been turned in the wrong direction, and is looking away from the truth?

[**Glaucon**] Yes, he said, such an art may be presumed.

[**Socrates**] And whereas the other so-called virtues of the soul seem to be akin to bodily qualities, for even when they are not originally innate they can be implanted later by habit and exercise, the of wisdom more than anything else contains a divine element which always remains, and by this conversion is rendered useful and profitable; or, on the other hand, hurtful and useless. Did you never observe the narrow intelligence flashing from the keen eye of a clever rogue --how eager he is, how clearly his paltry soul sees the way to his end; he is the reverse of blind, but his keen eyesight is forced into the service of evil, and he is mischievous in proportion to his cleverness.

[**Glaucon**] Very true, he said.

[**Socrates**] But what if there had been a circumcision of such natures in the days of their youth; and they had been severed from those sensual pleasures, such as eating and drinking, which, like leaden weights, were attached to them at their birth, and which drag them down and turn the vision of their souls upon the things that are below -- if, I say, they had been released from these impediments and turned in the opposite direction, the very same faculty in them would have seen the truth as keenly as they see what their eyes are turned to now.

[**Glaucon**] Very likely.

[**Socrates**] Yes, I said; and there is another thing which is likely. or rather a necessary inference from what has preceded, that neither the uneducated and uninformed of the truth, nor yet those who never make an end of their education, will be able ministers of State; not the former, because they have no single aim of duty which is the rule of all their actions, private as well as public; nor the latter, because they will not act at all except upon compulsion, fancying that they are already dwelling apart in the islands of the blest.

[**Glaucon**] Very true, he replied.

[**Socrates**] Then, I said, the business of us who are the founders of the State will be to compel the best minds to attain that knowledge which we have already shown to be the greatest of all- they must continue to ascend until they arrive at the good; but when they have ascended and seen enough we must not allow them to do as they do now.

[**Glaucon**] What do you mean?

[**Socrates**] I mean that they remain in the upper world: but this must not be allowed; they must be made to descend again among the prisoners in the cave, and partake of their labors and honors, whether they are worth having or not.

[**Glaucon**] But is not this unjust? he said; ought we to give them a worse life, when they might have a better?

[**Socrates**] You have again forgotten, my friend, I said, the intention of the legislator, who did not aim at making any one class in the State happy above the rest; the happiness was to be in the whole State, and he held the citizens together by persuasion and necessity, making them benefactors of the State, and therefore benefactors of one another; to this end he created them, not to please themselves, but to be his instruments in binding up the State.

[**Glaucon**] True, he said, I had forgotten.

[**Socrates**] Observe, Glaucon, that there will be no injustice in compelling our philosophers to have a care and providence of others; we shall explain to them that in other States, men of their class are not obliged to share in the toils of politics: and this is reasonable, for they grow up at their own sweet will, and the government would rather not have them. Being self-taught, they cannot be expected to show any gratitude for a culture which they have never received. But we have brought you into the world to be rulers of the hive, kings of yourselves and of the other citizens, and have educated you far better and more perfectly than they have been educated, and you are better able to share in the double duty. Wherefore each of you, when his turn comes, must go down to the general underground abode, and get the habit of seeing in the dark. When you have acquired the habit, you will see ten thousand times better than the inhabitants of the cave, and you will know what the several images are, and what they represent, because you have seen the beautiful and just and good in their truth. And thus our State which is also yours will be a reality, and not a dream only, and will be administered in a spirit unlike that of other States, in which men fight with one another about shadows only and are distracted in the struggle for power, which in their eyes is a great good. Whereas the truth is that the State in which the rulers are most reluctant to govern is always the best and most quietly governed, and the State in which they are most eager, the worst.

[**Glaucon**] Quite true, he replied.

[**Socrates**] And will our pupils, when they hear this, refuse to take their turn at the toils of State, when they are allowed to spend the greater part of their time with one another in the heavenly light?

[**Glaucon**] Impossible, he answered; for they are just men, and the commands which we impose upon them are just; there can be no doubt that every one of them will take office as a stern necessity, and not after the fashion of our present rulers of State.

[**Socrates**] Yes, my friend, I said; and there lies the point. You must contrive for your future rulers another and a better life than that of a ruler, and then you may have a well-ordered State; for only in the State which offers this, will they rule who are truly rich, not in silver and gold, but in virtue and wisdom, which are the true blessings of life. Whereas if they go to the administration of public affairs, poor and hungering after the' own private advantage, thinking that hence they are to snatch the chief good, order there can never be; for they will be fighting about office, and the civil and domestic broils which thus arise will be the ruin of the rulers themselves and of the whole State.

[**Glaucon**] Most true, he replied.

[**Socrates**] And the only life which looks down upon the life of political ambition is that of true philosophy. Do you know of any other?

[**Glaucon**] Indeed, I do not, he said.

[**Socrates**] And those who govern ought not to be lovers of the task? For, if they are, there will be rival lovers, and they will fight.

[**Glaucon**] No question.

[**Socrates**] Who then are those whom we shall compel to be guardians? Surely they will be the men who are wisest about affairs of State, and by whom the State is best administered, and who at the same time have other honors and another and a better life than that of politics?

[**Glaucon**] They are the men, and I will choose them, he replied.

[**Socrates**] And now shall we consider in what way such guardians will be produced, and how they are to be brought from darkness to light, -- as some are said to have ascended from the world below to the gods?

[**Glaucon**] By all means, he replied.

[**Socrates**] The process, I said, is not the turning over of an oyster-shell, but the turning round of a soul passing from a day which is little better than night to the true day of being, that is, the ascent from below, which we affirm to be true philosophy?

[**Glaucon**] Quite so.

Source: Indiana Wesleyan University

https://www.indwes.edu/academics/jwhc/_files/plato_s%20allegory%20of%20the%20cave.pdf

VR NOTES 2

Virtual Philosophy

Professor Lane's Course Using VR Technology

ASSIGNMENT MODULE THREE | ORIGINAL SCULPTURE

SCULPTR APPLICATION

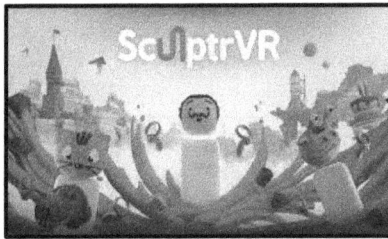

INSTRUCTIONS: After closely reading the following unusual essay, create a piece of original SCULPTURE or IMPRESSION that can accompany the text and brings out the proper VISION of what the author (Jorge Borges) was trying to convey. Do this by using the SCULPT application on your VR headset. There is a learning curve, but you don't need any prior training in sculpture to create a unique vision, building, landscape, or unique landscape. Be as creative as you wish to be, but the key is that your SCULPT piece should reflect to some degree the content and/or the environment that is inherent in the essay from Borges' LIBRARY OF BABEL. Experiment and you can do more than one SCULPT presentation. After you have finished your piece, export it and place it on your website and/or a direct link to it that others can then enjoy. If it is interactive, then make sure to capture it via video and export it as such.

THE LIBRARY OF BABEL
by Jorge Luis Borges (1941)

By this art you may contemplate the variations of the 23 letters...

The Anatomy of Melancholy, part 2, sect. II, mem. IV

The universe (which others call the Library) is composed of an indefinite and perhaps infinite number of hexagonal galleries, with vast air shafts between, surrounded by very low railings. From any of the hexagons one can see, interminably, the upper and lower floors. The distribution of the galleries is invariable. Twenty shelves, five long shelves per side, cover all the sides except two; their height, which is the distance from floor to ceiling, scarcely exceeds that of a normal bookcase. One of the free sides leads to a narrow hallway which opens onto another gallery, identical to the first and to all the rest. To the left and right of the hallway there are two very small closets. In the first, one may sleep standing up; in the other, satisfy one's fecal necessities. Also through here passes a spiral stairway, which sinks abysmally and soars upwards to remote distances. In the hallway there is a mirror which faithfully duplicates all appearances. Men usually infer from this mirror that the Library is not infinite (if it were, why this illusory duplication?); I prefer to dream that its polished surfaces represent and promise the infinite ... Light is provided by some spherical fruit which bear the name of lamps. There are two, transversally placed, in each hexagon. The light they emit is insufficient, incessant.

Like all men of the Library, I have traveled in my youth; I have wandered in search of a book, perhaps the catalogue of catalogues; now that my eyes can hardly decipher what I write, I am preparing to die just a few leagues from the hexagon in which I was born. Once I am dead, there will be no lack of pious hands to throw me over the railing; my grave will be the fathomless air; my body will sink endlessly and decay and dissolve in the wind generated by the fall, which is infinite. I say that the Library is unending. The idealists argue that the hexagonal rooms are a necessary form of absolute space or, at least, of our intuition of space. They reason that a triangular or pentagonal room is inconceivable. (The mystics claim that their ecstasy reveals to them a circular chamber containing a great circular book, whose spine is continuous and which follows the complete circle of the walls; but their testimony is suspect; their words, obscure. This cyclical book is God.) Let it suffice now for me to repeat the classic dictum: *The Library is a sphere whose exact center is any one of its hexagons and whose circumference is inaccessible.*

There are five shelves for each of the hexagon's walls; each shelf contains thirty-five books of uniform format; each book is of four hundred and ten pages; each page, of forty lines, each line, of some eighty letters which are black in color. There are also letters on the spine of each book; these letters do not indicate or prefigure what the pages will say. I know that this incoherence at one time seemed mysterious. Before summarizing the solution (whose discovery, in spite of its tragic projections, is perhaps the capital fact in history) I wish to recall a few axioms.

First: The Library exists *ab aeterno*. This truth, whose immediate corollary is the future eternity of the world, cannot be placed in doubt by any reasonable mind. Man, the imperfect librarian, may be the product of chance or of malevolent demiurgi; the universe, with its elegant endowment of shelves, of enigmatical volumes, of inexhaustible stairways for the traveler and latrines for the seated librarian, can only be the work of a god. To perceive the distance between the divine and the human, it is enough to compare these crude wavering symbols which my fallible hand scrawls on the cover of a book, with the organic letters inside: punctual, delicate, perfectly black, inimitably symmetrical.

Second: *The orthographical symbols are twenty-five in number.*[1] This finding

made it possible, three hundred years ago, to formulate a general theory of the Library and solve satisfactorily the problem which no conjecture had deciphered: the formless and chaotic nature of almost all the books. One which my father saw in a hexagon on circuit fifteen ninety-four was made up of the letters MCV, perversely repeated from the first line to the last. Another (very much consulted in this area) is a mere labyrinth of letters, but the next-to-last page says *Oh time thy pyramids*. This much is already known: for every sensible line of straightforward statement, there are leagues of senseless cacophonies, verbal jumbles and incoherences. (I know of an uncouth region whose librarians repudiate the vain and superstitious custom of finding a meaning in books and equate it with that of finding a meaning in dreams or in the chaotic lines of one's palm ... They admit that the inventors of this writing imitated the twenty-five natural symbols, but maintain that this application is accidental and that the books signify nothing in themselves. This dictum, we shall see, is not entirely fallacious.)

For a long time it was believed that these impenetrable books corresponded to past or remote languages. It is true that the most ancient men, the first librarians, used a language quite different from the one we now speak; it is true that a few miles to the right the tongue is dialectical and that ninety floors farther up, it is incomprehensible. All this, I repeat, is true, but four hundred and ten pages of inalterable MCV's cannot correspond to any language, no matter how dialectical or rudimentary it may be. Some insinuated that each letter could influence the following one and that the value of MCV in the third line of page 71 was not the one the same series may have in another position on another page, but this vague thesis did not prevail. Others thought of cryptographs; generally, this conjecture has been accepted, though not in the sense in which it was formulated by its originators.

Five hundred years ago, the chief of an upper hexagon[2] came upon a book as confusing as the others, but which had nearly two pages of homogeneous lines. He showed his find to a wandering decoder who told him the lines were written in Portuguese; others said they were Yiddish. Within a century, the language was established: a Samoyedic Lithuanian dialect of Guarani, with classical Arabian inflections. The content was also deciphered: some notions of combinative analysis, illustrated with examples of variations with unlimited repetition. These examples made it possible for a librarian of genius to discover the fundamental law of the Library. This thinker observed that all the books, no matter how diverse they might be, are made up of the same elements: the space, the period, the comma, the twenty-two letters of the alphabet. He also alleged a fact which travelers have confirmed: *In the vast Library there are no two identical books.* From these two incontrovertible premises he deduced that the Library is total and that its shelves register all the possible combinations of the twenty-odd orthographical symbols (a number which, though extremely vast, is not infinite): Everything: the minutely detailed history of the future, the archangels' autobiographies, the faithful catalogues of the Library, thousands and thousands of false catalogues, the demonstration of the fallacy of those catalogues, the demonstration of the fallacy of the true catalogue, the Gnostic gospel of Basilides, the commentary on that gospel, the commentary on the commentary on that gospel, the true story of your death, the translation of every book in all languages, the interpolations of every book in all books.

When it was proclaimed that the Library contained all books, the first impression was one of extravagant happiness. All men felt themselves to be the masters of an intact and secret treasure. There was no personal or world problem whose eloquent solution did not exist in some hexagon. The universe was justified, the universe suddenly usurped the unlimited dimensions of hope. At that time a great deal was said about the Vindications: books of apology and prophecy which vindicated for all time the acts of every man in the universe and retained prodigious arcana for his future. Thousands of the greedy abandoned their sweet native hexagons and rushed up the stairways, urged on by the vain intention of finding their Vindication. These pilgrims disputed in the narrow corridors, proferred dark curses, strangled each other on the divine stairways, flung the deceptive books into the air shafts, met their death cast down in a similar fashion by the inhabitants of remote regions. Others went mad ... The Vindications exist (I have seen two which refer to persons of the future, to persons who are perhaps not imaginary) but the searchers did not remember that the possibility of a man's finding his Vindication, or some treacherous variation thereof, can be computed as zero.

At that time it was also hoped that a clarification of humanity's basic mysteries -- the origin of the Library and of time -- might be found. It is verisimilar that these grave mysteries could be explained in words: if the language of philosophers is not sufficient, the multiform Library will have produced the unprecedented language required, with its vocabularies and grammars. For four centuries now men have exhausted the hexagons ... There are official searchers, *inquisitors*. I have seen them in the performance of their function: they always arrive extremely tired from their journeys; they speak of a broken stairway which almost killed them; they talk with the librarian of galleries and stairs; sometimes they pick up the nearest volume and leaf through it, looking for infamous words. Obviously, no one expects to discover anything.

As was natural, this inordinate hope was followed by an excessive depression. The certitude that some shelf in some hexagon held precious books and that these precious books were inaccessible, seemed almost intolerable. A blasphemous sect suggested that the searches should cease and that all men should juggle letters and symbols until they constructed, by an

improbable gift of chance, these canonical books. The
authorities were obliged to issue severe orders. The sect
disappeared, but in my childhood I have seen old men
who, for long periods of time, would hide in the latrines
with some metal disks in a forbidden dice cup and feebly
mimic the divine disorder.

Others, inversely, believed that it was fundamental to
eliminate useless

works. They invaded the hexagons, showed credentials
which were not always false, leafed through a volume
with displeasure and condemned whole shelves: their
hygienic, ascetic furor caused the senseless perdition of
millions of books. Their name is execrated, but those
who deplore the ``treasures'' destroyed by this frenzy
neglect two notable facts. One: the Library is so
enormous that any reduction of human origin is
infinitesimal. The other: every copy is unique,
irreplaceable, but (since the Library is total) there are
always several hundred thousand imperfect facsimiles:
works which differ only in a letter or a comma. Counter
to general opinion, I venture to suppose that the
consequences of the Purifiers' depredations have been
exaggerated by the horror these fanatics produced. They
were urged on by the delirium of trying to reach the
books in the Crimson Hexagon: books whose format is
smaller than usual, all-powerful, illustrated and magical.

We also know of another superstition of that time:
that of the Man of the Book. On some shelf in some
hexagon (men reasoned) there must exist a book which
is the formula and perfect compendium *of all the rest:*
some librarian has gone through it and he is analogous to

a god. In the language of this zone vestiges of this remote functionary's cult still persist. Many wandered in search of Him. For a century they have exhausted in vain the most varied areas. How could one locate the venerated and secret hexagon which housed Him? Someone proposed a regressive method: To locate book A, consult first book B which indicates A's position; to locate book B, consult first a book C, and so on to infinity ... In adventures such as these, I have squandered and wasted my years. It does not seem unlikely to me that there is a total book on some shelf of the universe[3]; I pray to the unknown gods that a man -- just one, even though it were thousands of years ago! -- may have examined and read it. If honor and wisdom and happiness are not for me, let them be for others. Let heaven exist, though my place be in hell. Let me be outraged and annihilated, but for one instant, in one being, let Your enormous Library be justified. The impious maintain that nonsense is normal in the Library and that the reasonable (and even humble and pure coherence) is an almost miraculous exception. They speak (I know) of the ``feverish Library whose chance volumes are constantly in danger of changing into others and affirm, negate and confuse everything like a delirious divinity." These words, which not only denounce the disorder but exemplify it as well, notoriously prove their authors' abominable taste and desperate ignorance. In truth, the Library includes all verbal structures, all variations permitted by the twenty-five orthographical symbols, but not a single example of absolute nonsense. It is useless to observe that the best volume of the many hexagons under my administration is entitled *The Combed Thunderclap* and another *The Plaster Cramp* and another *Axaxaxas mlö*. These phrases, at first glance incoherent, can no doubt be justified in a cryptographical or allegorical manner; such a justification is verbal and, *ex hypothesi,* already figures in the Library. I cannot combine some characters *dhcmrlchtdj* which the divine Library has not foreseen and which in one of its secret tongues do not contain a terrible meaning. No one can articulate a syllable which is not filled with tenderness and fear, which is not, in one of these languages, the powerful name of a god. To speak is to fall into tautology. This wordy and useless epistle already exists in one of the thirty volumes of the five shelves of one of the innumerable hexagons -- and its refutation as well. (An *n* number of possible languages use the same vocabulary; in some of them, the symbol *library* allows the correct definition *a ubiquitous and lasting system of hexagonal galleries,* but *library* is *bread* or *pyramid* or anything else, and these seven words which define it have another value. You who read me, are You sure of understanding my language?)

The methodical task of writing distracts me from the present state of men. The certitude that everything has been written negates us or turns us into phantoms. I know of districts in which the young men prostrate themselves before books and kiss their pages in a barbarous manner, but they do not know how to decipher a single letter. Epidemics, heretical conflicts, peregrinations which inevitably degenerate into banditry, have decimated the population. I believe I have mentioned suicides, more and more frequent with the years. Perhaps my old age and fearfulness deceive me, but I suspect that the human species -- the unique species -- is about to be extinguished, but the Library will endure: illuminated, solitary, infinite, perfectly motionless, equipped with precious volumes, useless, incorruptible, secret.

I have just written the word "infinite".' I have not interpolated this adjective out of rhetorical habit; I say that it is not illogical to think that the world is infinite. Those who judge it to be limited postulate that in remote places the corridors and stairways and hexagons can conceivably come to an end -- which is absurd. Those who imagine it to be without limit forget that the possible number of books does have such a limit. I venture to suggest this solution to the ancient problem: *The Library is unlimited and cyclical.* If an eternal traveler were to cross it in any direction, after centuries he would see that the same volumes were repeated in the same disorder (which, thus repeated, would be an order: the Order). My solitude is gladdened by this elegant hope[4].

Translated by J. E. I.

1 The original manuscript does not contain digits or capital letters. The punctuation has been limited to the comma and the period. These two signs, the space and the twenty-two letters of the alphabet are the twenty-five symbols considered sufficient by this unknown author. *(Editor's note.)*

2 Before, there was a man for every three hexagons. Suicide and pulmonary diseases have destroyed that proportion. A memory of unspeakable melancholy: at times I have traveled for many nights through corridors and along polished stairways without finding a single librarian.

3 I repeat: it suffices that a book be possible for it to exist. Only the impossible is excluded. For example: no book can be a ladder, although no doubt there are books which discuss and negate and demonstrate this possibility and others whose structure corresponds to that of a ladder.

4 Letizia Álvarez de Toledo has observed that this vast Library is useless: rigorously speaking, *a single volume* would be sufficient, a

volume of ordinary format, printed in nine or ten point type, containing an infinite number if infinitely thin leaves. (In the early seventeenth century, Cavalieri said that all solid bodies are the superimposition of an infinite number of planes.) The handling of this silky vade mecum would not be convenient: each apparent page would unfold into other analogous ones; the inconceivable middle page would have no reverse.

Source:

https://www.sccs.swarthmore.edu/users/oo/pwillen1/lit/babel.htm

VR NOTES 3

Virtual Philosophy

Professor Lane's Course Using VR Technology

ASSIGNMENT MODULE FOUR | MEDITATION

TRIPPVR APPLICATION

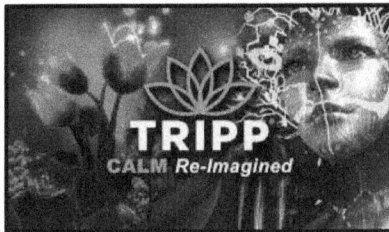

INSTRUCTIONS: After closely reading the following meditational text by Sri Ramana Maharshi ("Who Am I"?), reflect on the ideas that he presents concerning "Self-Enquiry" while using the TRIPP meditational application. Feel free to choose any journey within the application and let your mind go inward as you think about what you read. After you are finished, write a 250 essay about what you experienced and what does Ramana and Socrates mean by "Know thyself by thyself." Post the essay on your website and be sure to share it with your classmates via Canvas.

WHO AM I?

(Nan Yar?)

Ramana Maharshi

As all living beings desire to be happy always, without misery, as in the case of everyone there is observed supreme love for one's self, and as happiness alone is the cause for love, in order to gain that happiness which is one's nature and which is experienced in the state of deep sleep where there is no mind, one should know one's self. For that, the path of knowledge, the inquiry of the form "Who am I?", is the principal means.

1. *Who am I?*

   The gross body which is composed of the seven humours (dhatus), I am not; the five cognitive sense organs, viz. the senses of hearing, touch, sight, taste, and smell, which apprehend their respective objects, viz. sound, touch, colour, taste, and odour, I am not; the five cognitive sense- organs, viz. the organs of speech, locomotion, grasping, excretion, and procreation, which have as their respective functions speaking, moving, grasping, excreting, and enjoying, I am not; the five vital airs, prana, etc., which perform respectively the five functions of in-breathing, etc., I am not; even the mind which thinks, I am not; the nescience too, which is endowed only with the residual impressions of objects, and in which there are no objects and no functioning's, I am not.

2. *If I am none of these, then who am I?*

   After negating all of the above-mentioned as 'not this', 'not this', that Awareness which alone remains - that I am.

3. *What is the nature of Awareness?*
The nature of Awareness is existence-consciousness-bliss

4. *When will the realization of the Self be gained?*
When the world which is what-is-seen has been removed, there will be realization of the Self which is the seer.

5. *Will there not be realization of the Self even while the world is there (taken as real)?*
There will not be.

6. *Why?*
The seer and the object seen are like the rope and the snake. Just as the knowledge of the rope which is the substrate will not arise unless the false knowledge of the illusory serpent goes, so the realization of the Self which is the substrate will not be gained unless the belief that the world is real is removed.

7. *When will the world which is the object seen be removed?*
When the mind, which is the cause of all cognition's and of all actions, becomes quiescent, the world will disappear.

8. *What is the nature of the mind?*
What is called 'mind' is a wondrous power residing in the Self. It causes all thoughts to arise. Apart from thoughts, there is no such thing as mind. Therefore, thought is the nature of mind. Apart from thoughts, there is no independent entity called the world. In deep sleep there are no thoughts, and there is no world. In the states of waking and dream, there are

thoughts, and there is a world also. Just as the spider emits the thread (of the web) out of itself and again withdraws it into itself, likewise the mind projects the world out of itself and again resolves it into itself. When the mind comes out of the Self, the world appears. Therefore, when the world appears (to be real), the Self does not appear; and when the Self appears (shines) the world does not appear. When one persistently inquires into the nature of the mind, the mind will end leaving the Self (as the residue). What is referred to as the Self is the Atman. The mind always exists only in dependence on something gross; it cannot stay alone. It is the mind that is called the subtle body or the soul (jiva).

9. *What is the path of inquiry for understanding the nature of the mind?*
   That which rises as 'I' in this body is the mind. If one inquires as to where in the body the thought 'I' rises first, one would discover that it rises in the heart. That is the place of the mind's origin. Even if one thinks constantly 'I' 'I', one will be led to that place. Of all the thoughts that arise in the mind, the 'I' thought is the first. It is only after the rise of this that the other thoughts arise. It is after the appearance of the first personal pronoun that the second and third personal pronouns appear; without the first personal pronoun there will not be the second and third.

10. *How will the mind become quiescent?*
    By the inquiry 'Who am I?'. The thought 'who am I?' will destroy all other thoughts, and like the stick used for stirring the burning pyre, it will itself in the end get destroyed. Then, there will arise Self-realization.

11. *What is the means for constantly holding on to the thought 'Who am I?'*

    When other thoughts arise, one should not pursue them, but should inquire: 'To whom do they arise?' It does not matter how many thoughts arise. As each thought arises, one should inquire with diligence, "To whom has this thought arisen?". The answer that would emerge would be "To me". Thereupon if one inquires "Who am I?", the mind will go back to its source; and the thought that arose will become quiescent. With repeated practice in this manner, the mind will develop the skill to stay in its source. When the mind that is subtle goes out through the brain and the sense- organs, the gross names and forms appear; when it stays in the heart, the names and forms disappear. Not letting the mind go out, but retaining it in the Heart is what is called "inwardness" (antar-mukha). Letting the mind go out of the Heart is known as "externalisation" (bahir-mukha). Thus, when the mind stays in the Heart, the 'I' which is the source of all thoughts will go, and the Self which ever exists will shine. Whatever one does, one should do without the egoity "I". If one acts in that way, all will appear as of the nature of Siva (God).

12. *Are there no other means for making the mind quiescent?*

    Other than inquiry, there are no adequate means. If through other means it is sought to control the mind, the mind will appear to be controlled, but will again go forth. Through the control of breath also, the mind will become quiescent; but it will be quiescent only so long as the breath remains controlled, and when the breath resumes the mind also will again start moving and will wander as impelled by residual impressions. The source is the same for both mind and breath. Thought, indeed, is the nature of the mind. The thought "I" is the first thought of the mind; and that is egoity. It is from that whence egoity originates that breath also originates. Therefore, when the mind becomes quiescent, the breath is controlled, and when the breath is controlled the mind becomes quiescent. But in deep sleep, although the mind becomes quiescent, the breath does not stop. This is because of the will of God, so that the body may be preserved and other people may not be under the impression that it is dead. In the state of waking and in samadhi, when the mind becomes quiescent the breath is controlled. Breath is the gross form of mind. Till the time of death, the mind keeps breath in the body; and when the body dies the mind takes the breath along with it. Therefore, the exercise of breath-control is only an aid for rendering the mind quiescent (manonigraha); it will not destroy the mind (manonasa). Like the practice of breath-control. meditation on the forms of God, repetition of mantras, restriction on food, etc., are but aids for rendering the mind quiescent. Through meditation on the forms of God and through repetition of mantras, the mind becomes one- pointed. The mind will always be wandering. Just as when a chain is given to an elephant to hold in its trunk it will go along grasping the chain and nothing else, so also when the mind is occupied with a name or form it will grasp that alone. When the mind expands in the form of countless thoughts, each thought becomes weak; but as thoughts get resolved the mind becomes one-pointed and strong; for such a mind Self-inquiry will become easy. Of all the restrictive rules, that relating to the taking of sattvic food in moderate quantities is the best; by observing this rule, the sattvic quality of mind will increase, and that will be helpful to Self-inquiry.

13. *The residual impressions (thoughts) of objects appear wending like the waves of an ocean. When will all of them get destroyed?*
As the meditation on the Self rises higher and higher, the thoughts will get destroyed.

14. *Is it possible for the residual impressions of objects that come from beginningless time, as it were, to be resolved, and for one to remain as the pure Self?*
Without yielding to the doubt "Is it possible, or not?", one should persistently hold on to the meditation on the Self. Even if one be a great sinner, one should not worry and weep "O! I am a sinner, how can I be saved?"; one should completely renounce the thought "I am a sinner"; and concentrate keenly on meditation on the Self; then, one would surely succeed. There are not two minds - one good and the other evil; the mind is only one. It is the residual impressions that are of two kinds - auspicious and inauspicious. When the mind is under the influence of auspicious impressions it is called good; and when it is under the influence of inauspicious impressions it is regarded as evil. The mind should not be allowed to wander towards worldly objects and what concerns other people. However bad other people may be, one should bear no hatred for them. Both desire and hatred should be eschewed. All that one gives to others one gives to one's self. If this truth is understood who will not give to others? When one's self arises all arises; when one's self becomes quiescent all becomes quiescent. To the extent we

behave with humility, to that extent there will result good. If the mind is rendered quiescent, one may live anywhere.

15. *How long should inquiry be practised?*
As long as there are impressions of objects in the mind, so long the inquiry "Who am I?" is required. As thoughts arise they should be destroyed then and there in the very place of their origin, through inquiry. If one resorts to contemplation of the Self unintermittently, until the Self is gained, that alone would do. As long as there are enemies within the fortress, they will continue to sally forth; if they are destroyed as they emerge, the fortress will fall into our hands.

16. *What is the nature of the Self?*
What exists in truth is the Self alone. The world, the individual soul, and God are appearances in it. like silver in mother-of-pearl, these three appear at the same time, and disappear at the same time. The Self is that where there is absolutely no "I" thought. That is called "Silence". The Self itself is the world; the Self itself is "I"; the Self itself is God; all is Siva, the Self.

17. *Is not everything the work of God?*
Without desire, resolve, or effort, the sun rises; and in its mere presence, the sun-stone emits fire, the lotus blooms, water evaporates; people perform their various functions and then rest. Just as in the presence of the magnet the needle moves, it is by virtue of the mere presence of God that the souls governed by the three (cosmic) functions or the fivefold divine activity perform their actions and then rest, in accordance with their respective karmas. God has no resolve; no karma

attaches itself to Him. That is like worldly actions not affecting the sun, or like the merits and demerits of the other four elements not affecting all pervading space.

18. *Of the devotees, who is the greatest?*
He who gives himself up to the Self that is God is the most excellent devotee. Giving one's self up to God means remaining constantly in the Self without giving room for the rise of any thoughts other than that of the Self. Whatever burdens are thrown on God, He bears them. Since the supreme power of God makes all things move, why should we, without submitting ourselves to it, constantly worry ourselves with thoughts as to what should be done and how, and what should not be done and how not? We know that the train carries all loads, so after getting on it why should we carry our small luggage on our head to our discomfort, instead of putting it down in the train and feeling at ease?

19. *What is non-attachment?*
As thoughts arise, destroying them utterly without any residue in the very place of their origin is non-attachment. Just as the pearl-diver ties a stone to his waist, sinks to the bottom of the sea and there takes the pearls, so each one of us should be endowed with non-attachment, dive within oneself and obtain the Self-Pearl.

20. *Is it not possible for God and the Guru to effect the release of a soul?*
God and the Guru will only show the way to release; they will not by themselves take the soul to the state of release. In truth, God and the Guru are not different.

Just as the prey which has fallen into the jaws of a tiger has no escape, so those who have come within the ambit of the Guru's gracious look will be saved by the Guru and will not get lost; yet, each one should by his own effort pursue the path shown by God or Guru and gain release. One can know oneself only with one's own eye of knowledge, and not with somebody else's. Does he who is Rama require the help of a mirror to know that he is Rama?

21. *Is it necessary for one who longs for release to inquire into the nature of categories (tattvas)?*
Just as one who wants to throw away garbage has no need to analyse it and see what it is, so one who wants to know the Self has no need to count the number of categories or inquire into their characteristics; what he has to do is to reject altogether the categories that hide the Self. The world should be considered like a dream.

22. *Is there no difference between waking and dream?*
Waking is long and a dream short; other than this there is no difference. Just as waking happenings seem real while awake. so do those in a dream while dreaming. In dream the mind takes on another body. In both waking and dream states thoughts. names and forms occur simultaneously.

23. *Is it any use reading books for those who long for release?*
All the texts say that in order to gain release one should render the mind quiescent; therefore their conclusive teaching is that the mind should be rendered quiescent; once this has been understood there is no need for endless reading. In order to quieten the mind

one has only to inquire within oneself what one's Self is; how could this search be done in books? One should know one's Self with one's own eye of wisdom. The Self is within the five sheaths; but books are outside them. Since the Self has to be inquired into by discarding the five sheaths, it is futile to search for it in books. There will come a time when one will have to forget all that one has learned.

24. *What is happiness?*
Happiness is the very nature of the Self; happiness and the Self are not different. There is no happiness in any object of the world. We imagine through our ignorance that we derive happiness from objects. When the mind goes out, it experiences misery. In truth, when its desires are fulfilled, it returns to its own place and enjoys the happiness that is the Self. Similarly, in the states of sleep, samadhi and fainting, and when the object desired is obtained or the object disliked is removed, the mind becomes inward-turned, and enjoys pure Self-Happiness. Thus the mind moves without rest alternately going out of the Self and returning to it. Under the tree the shade is pleasant; out in the open the heat is scorching. A person who has been going about in the sun feels cool when he reaches the shade. Someone who keeps on going from the shade into the sun and then back into the shade is a fool. A wise man stays permanently in the shade. Similarly, the mind of the one who knows the truth does not leave Brahman. The mind of the ignorant, on the contrary, revolves in the world, feeling miserable, and for a little time returns to Brahman to experience happiness. In fact, what is called the world is only thought. When the world disappears, i.e. when there is

no thought, the mind experiences happiness; and when the world appears, it goes through misery.

25. *What is wisdom-insight (jnana-drsti)?*
Remaining quiet is what is called wisdom-insight. To remain quiet is to resolve the mind in the Self. Telepathy, knowing past, present and future happenings and clairvoyance do not constitute wisdom-insight.

26. *What is the relation between desirelessness and wisdom?*
Desirelessness is wisdom. The two are not different; they are the same. Desirelessness is refraining from turning the mind towards any object. Wisdom means the appearance of no object. In other words, not seeking what is other than the Self is detachment or desirelessness; not leaving the Self is wisdom.

27. *What is the difference between inquiry and meditation?*
Inquiry consists in retaining the mind in the Self. Meditation consists in thinking that one's self is Brahman, existence-consciousness-bliss.

28. *What is release?*
Inquiring into the nature of one's self that is in bondage, and realising one's true nature is release.

Source:
https://drive.google.com/file/d/107yKFpXFwkuCON7ep
vx2C8tb-TZrBf4d/view

SRI RAMANARPANAM ASTU

VR NOTES 4

Virtual Philosophy

Professor Lane's Course Using VR Technology

ASSIGNMENT MODULE FIVE | CRITICAL THINKING

THE ROOM VR APPLICATION

INSTRUCTIONS: After closely reading the following essays, then enter the *Room VR: A Dark Matter* app on your VR headset. It is a complicated detective story and you will have to use your critical thinking skills, your patience, and the clues that it gives you to solve the mystery. Take your time and don't get frustrated. Half the fun is not getting it right at first and then figuring out why you are mistaken. Then you can try another pathway and succeed. This is one of the very highest rated VR games in the world and it was the one that convinced me that virtual reality is in our future. After you have solved the game and unraveled the secret (it will take several hours; enjoy the process since there is no need to rush), then write a 250 (or more) reaction piece about your experience, focusing on where you were misled or made the wrong choices and concentrating on those moments where you had an "aha" experience and solved one of the many puzzles embedded in the game. As the Nobel

Prize winner, Richard Feynman, often argued: it is important to acknowledge our mistakes and to learn from them. Oftentimes in school we are not allowed to fail, since the consequences are so severe. Here in this game, you get to try and try again until you succeed. Don't write your essay until you have completed and succeeded in the game. Good luck fellow detectives. Post your essay on your website and send a link directly to your professor at dlane@mtsac.edu. Place the essay under the title THE ROOM VR. In addition to Feynman's speech, read and re-read Carl Sagan's famous "Baloney Detection Kit."

CARGO CULT SCIENCE
Richard P.. Feynman

Some remarks on science, pseudoscience, and learning how to not fool yourself. Caltech's 1974 commencement address.

During the Middle Ages there were all kinds of crazy ideas, such as that a piece of rhinoceros horn would increase potency. (Another crazy idea of the Middle Ages is these hats we have on today—which is too loose in my case.) Then a method was discovered for separating the ideas—which was to try one to see if it worked, and if it didn't work, to eliminate it. This method became organized, of course, into science. And it developed very well, so that we are now in the scientific age. It is such a scientific age, in fact, that we have difficulty in understanding how witch doctors could *ever* have existed, when nothing that they proposed ever really worked—or very little of it did.

But even today I meet lots of people who sooner or later get me into a conversation about UFO's, or astrology, or some form of mysticism, expanded consciousness, new types of awareness, ESP, and so forth. And I've concluded that it's *not* a scientific world.

Most people believe so many wonderful things that I decided to investigate why they did. And what has been referred to as my curiosity for investigation has landed me in a difficulty where I found so much junk to talk about that I can't do it in this talk. I'm overwhelmed. First I started out by investigating various ideas of mysticism, and mystic experiences. I went into isolation tanks (they're dark and quiet and you float in Epsom salts) and got many hours of hallucinations, so I know something about that. Then I went to Esalen, which is a hotbed of this kind of thought (it's a wonderful place; you should go visit there). Then I became overwhelmed. I didn't realize how *much* there was.

I was sitting, for example, in a hot bath and there's another guy and a girl in the bath. He says to the girl, "I'm learning massage and I wonder if I could practice on you?" She says OK, so she gets up on a table and he starts off on her foot— working on her big toe and pushing it around. Then he turns to what is apparently his instructor, and says, "I feel a kind of dent. Is that the pituitary?" And she says, "No, that's not the way it feels." I say, "You're a hell of a long way from the pituitary, man." And they both looked at me—I had blown my cover, you see—and she said, "It's reflexology." So I closed my eyes and appeared to be meditating.

That's just an example of the kind of things that overwhelm me. I also looked into extrasensory perception and PSI phenomena, and the latest craze there was Uri Geller, a man who is supposed to be able to bend keys by rubbing them with his finger. So I went to his hotel room, on his invitation, to see a demonstration of both mind reading and bending keys. He didn't do any mind reading that succeeded; nobody can read my mind, I guess. And my boy held a key and Geller rubbed it, and nothing happened. Then he told us it works better under water, and so you can picture all of us standing in the bathroom with the water turned on and the key under it, and him rubbing the key with his finger. Nothing happened. So I was unable to investigate that phenomenon.

But then I began to think, what else is there that we believe? (And I thought then about the witch doctors, and how easy it would have been to check on them by noticing that nothing really worked.) So I found things that even more people believe, such as that we have some knowledge of how to educate. There are big schools of reading methods and mathematics methods, and so forth, but if you notice, you'll see the reading scores keep going down—or hardly going up—in spite of the fact that we continually use these same people to improve the methods. *There's* a witch doctor remedy that doesn't work. It ought to be looked into: how do they know that their method should work? Another example is how to treat criminals. We obviously have made no progress—lots of theory, but no progress—in decreasing the amount of crime by the method that we use to handle criminals.

Yet these things are said to be scientific. We study them. And I think ordinary people with commonsense ideas are intimidated by this pseudoscience. A teacher who has some good idea of how to teach her children to read is forced by the school system to do it some other way—or is even fooled by the school system into thinking that her method is not necessarily a good one. Or a parent of bad boys, after disciplining them in one way or another, feels guilty for the rest of her life because she didn't do "the right thing," according to the experts.

So we really ought to look into theories that don't work, and science that isn't science.

I tried to find a principle for discovering more of these kinds of things, and came up with the following system. Any time you find yourself in a conversation at a cocktail party—in which you do not feel uncomfortable that the hostess might come around and say, "Why are you fellows talking shop?" or that your wife will come around and say, "Why are you flirting again?"—then you can be sure you are talking about something about which nobody knows anything.

Using this method, I discovered a few more topics that I had forgotten—among them the efficacy of various forms of psychotherapy. So I began to investigate through the library, and so on, and I have so much to tell you that I can't do it at all. I will have to limit myself to just a few little things. I'll concentrate on the things more people believe in. Maybe I will give a series of speeches next year on all these subjects. It will take a long time.

I think the educational and psychological studies I mentioned are examples of what I would like to call Cargo Cult Science. In the South Seas there is a Cargo Cult of people. During the war they saw airplanes land with lots of good materials, and they want the same thing to happen now. So they've arranged to make things like runways, to put fires along the sides of the runways, to make a wooden hut for a man to sit in, with two wooden pieces on his head like headphones and bars of bamboo sticking out like antennas—he's the controller—and they wait for the airplanes to land. They're doing everything right. The form is perfect. It looks exactly the way it looked before. But it doesn't work. No airplanes land. So I call these things Cargo Cult Science, because they follow all the apparent precepts and forms of scientific investigation, but they're missing something essential, because the planes don't land.

Now it behooves me, of course, to tell you what they're missing. But it would he just about as difficult to explain to the South Sea Islanders how they have to arrange things so that they get some wealth in their system. It is not something simple like telling them how to improve the shapes of the earphones. But there is *one* feature I notice that is generally missing in Cargo Cult Science. That is the idea that we all hope you have learned in studying science in school—we never explicitly say what this *is*, but just hope that you catch on by all the examples of scientific investigation. It is interesting, therefore, to bring it out now and speak of it explicitly. It's a kind of scientific integrity, a principle of scientific thought that corresponds to a kind of utter honesty—a kind of leaning over backwards. For example, if you're doing an experiment, you should report everything that you think might make it invalid—not only what you think is right about it: other causes that could possibly explain your results; and things you thought of that you've eliminated by some other experiment, and how they worked—to make sure the other fellow can tell they have been eliminated.

Details that could throw doubt on your interpretation must be given, if you know them. You must do the best you can— if you know anything at all wrong, or possibly wrong—to explain it. If you make a theory, for example, and advertise it, or put it out, then you must also put down all the facts that disagree with it, as well as those that agree with it. There is also a more subtle problem. When you have put a lot of ideas together to make an elaborate theory, you want to make sure, when explaining what it fits, that those things it fits are not just the things that gave you the idea for the theory; but that the finished theory makes something else come out right, in addition.

In summary, the idea is to try to give *all* of the information to help others to judge the value of your contribution; not just the information that leads to judgment in one particular direction or another.

The easiest way to explain this idea is to contrast it, for example, with advertising. Last night I heard that Wesson Oil doesn't soak through food. Well, that's true. It's not dishonest; but the thing I'm talking about is not just a matter of not being dishonest, it's a matter of scientific integrity, which is another level. The fact that should be added to that advertising statement is that *no* oils soak through food, if operated at a certain temperature. If operated at another temperature, they *all* will—including Wesson Oil. So it's the implication which has been conveyed, not the fact, which is true, and the difference is what we have to deal with.

We've learned from experience that the truth will out. Other experimenters will repeat your experiment and find out whether you were wrong or right. Nature's phenomena will agree or they'll disagree with your theory. And, although you may gain some temporary fame and excitement, you will not gain a good reputation as a scientist if you haven't tried to be very careful in this kind of work. And it's this type of integrity, this kind of care not to fool yourself, that is missing to a large extent in much of the research in Cargo Cult Science.

A great deal of their difficulty is, of course, the difficulty of the subject and the inapplicability of the scientific method to the subject. Nevertheless, it should be remarked that this is not the only difficulty. That's *why* the planes don't land— but they don't land.

We have learned a lot from experience about how to handle some of the ways we fool ourselves. One example: Millikan measured the charge on an electron by an experiment with falling oil drops and got an answer which we now know not to be quite right. It's a little bit off, because he had the incorrect value for the viscosity of air. It's interesting to look at the history of measurements of the charge of the electron, after Millikan. If you plot them as a function of time, you find that one is a little bigger than Millikan's, and the next one's a little bit bigger than that, and the next one's a little bit bigger than that, until finally they settle down to a number which is higher.

Why didn't they discover that the new number was higher right away? It's a thing that scientists are ashamed of—this history—because it's apparent that people did things like this: When they got a number that was too high above Millikan's, they thought something must be wrong—and they would look for and find a reason why something might be wrong. When they got a number closer to Millikan's value they didn't look so hard. And so they eliminated the numbers that were too far off, and did other things like that. We've learned those tricks nowadays, and now we don't have that kind of a disease.

But this long history of learning how to not fool ourselves—of having utter scientific integrity—is, I'm sorry to say, something that we haven't specifically included in any particular course that I know of. We just hope you've caught on by osmosis.

The first principle is that you must not fool yourself—and you are the easiest person to fool. So you have to be very careful about that. After you've not fooled yourself, it's easy not to fool other scientists. You just have to be honest in a conventional way after that.

I would like to add something that's not essential to the science, but something I kind of believe, which is that you should not fool the layman when you're talking as a scientist. I'm not trying to tell you what to do about cheating on your wife, or fooling your girlfriend, or something like that, when you're not trying to be a scientist, but just trying to be an ordinary human being. We'll leave those problems up to you and your rabbi. I'm talking about a specific, extra type of integrity that is not lying, but bending over backwards to show how you're maybe wrong, that you ought to do when acting as a scientist. And this is our responsibility as scientists, certainly to other scientists, and I think to laymen.

For example, I was a little surprised when I was talking to a friend who was going to go on the radio. He does work on cosmology and astronomy, and he wondered how he would explain what the applications of this work were. "Well," I said, "there aren't any." He said, "Yes, but then we won't get support for more research of this kind." I think that's kind of dishonest. If you're representing yourself as a scientist, then you should explain to the layman what you're doing—

and if they don't want to support you under those circumstances, then that's their decision.

One example of the principle is this: If you've made up your mind to test a theory, or you want to explain some idea, you should always decide to publish it whichever way it comes out. If we only publish results of a certain kind, we can make the argument look good. We must publish *both* kinds of result. For example—let's take advertising again—suppose some particular cigarette has some particular property, like low nicotine. It's published widely by the company that this means it is good for you—they don't say, for instance, that the tars are a different proportion, or that something else is the matter with the cigarette. In other words, publication probability depends upon the answer. That should not be done.

I say that's also important in giving certain types of government advice. Supposing a senator asked you for advice about whether drilling a hole should be done in his state; and you decide it would be better in some other state. If you don't publish such a result, it seems to me you're not giving scientific advice. You're being used. If your answer happens to come out in the direction the government or the politicians like, they can use it as an argument in their favor; if it comes out the other way, they don't publish it at all. That's not giving scientific advice.

Other kinds of errors are more characteristic of poor science. When I was at Cornell. I often talked to the people in the psychology department. One of the students told me she wanted to do an experiment that went something like this—I don't remember it in detail, but it had been found by others that under certain circumstances, X, rats did something, A. She was curious as to whether, if she changed the circumstances to Y, they would still do, A. So her proposal was to do the experiment under circumstances Y and see if they still did A.

I explained to her that it was necessary first to repeat in her laboratory the experiment of the other person—to do it under condition X to see if she could also get result A—and then change to Y and see if A changed. Then she would know that the real difference was the thing she thought she had under control.

She was very delighted with this new idea, and went to her professor. And his reply was, no, you cannot do that, because the experiment has already been done and you would be wasting time. This was in about 1935 or so, and it seems to have been the general policy then to not try to repeat psychological experiments, but only to change the conditions and see what happens.

Nowadays there's a certain danger of the same thing happening, even in the famous field of physics. I was shocked to hear of an experiment done at the big accelerator at the National Accelerator Laboratory, where a person used deuterium. In order to compare his heavy hydrogen results to what might happen to light hydrogen he had to use data from someone else's experiment on light hydrogen, which was done on different apparatus. When asked he said it was because he couldn't get time on the program (because there's so little time and it's such expensive apparatus) to do the experiment with light hydrogen on this apparatus because there wouldn't be any new result. And so the men in charge of programs at NAL are so anxious for new results, in order to get more money to keep the thing going for public relations purposes, they are destroying—possibly—the value of the experiments themselves, which is the whole purpose of the thing. It is often hard for the experimenters there to complete their work as their scientific integrity demands.

All experiments in psychology are not of this type, however. For example, there have been many experiments running rats through all kinds of mazes, and so on—with little clear result. But in 1937 a man named Young did a very interesting one. He had a long corridor with doors all along one side where the rats came in, and doors along the other side where the food was. He wanted to see if he could train the rats to go in at the third door down from wherever he started them off. No. The rats went immediately to the door where the food had been the time before.

The question was, how did the rats know, because the corridor was so beautifully built and so uniform, that this was the same door as before? Obviously there was something about the door that was different from the other doors. So he painted the doors very carefully, arranging the textures on the faces of the doors exactly the same. Still the rats could tell. Then he thought maybe the rats were smelling the food, so he used chemicals to change the smell after each run. Still the rats could tell. Then he realized the rats might be able to tell by seeing the lights and the arrangement in the laboratory like any commonsense person. So he covered the corridor, and, still the rats could tell.

He finally found that they could tell by the way the floor sounded when they ran over it. And he could only fix that by putting his corridor in sand. So he covered one after another of all possible clues and finally was able to fool the rats so that they had to learn to go in the third door. If he relaxed any of his conditions, the rats could tell.

Now, from a scientific standpoint, that is an A-Number-1 experiment. That is the experiment that makes rat-running experiments sensible, because it uncovers the clues that the rat is really using—not what you think it's using. And that is the experiment that tells exactly what conditions you have to use in order to be careful and control everything in an experiment with rat-running.

I looked into the subsequent history of this research. The subsequent experiment, and the one after that, never referred to Mr. Young. They never used any of his criteria of putting the corridor on sand, or being very careful. They just went right on running rats in the same old way, and paid no attention to the great discoveries of Mr. Young, and his papers are not referred to, because he didn't discover anything about the rats. In fact, he discovered *all* the things you have to do to discover something about rats. But not paying attention to experiments like that is a characteristic of Cargo Cult Science.

Another example is the ESP experiments of Mr. Rhine, and other people. As various people have made criticisms—and they themselves have made criticisms of their own experiments—they improve the techniques so that the effects are smaller, and smaller, and smaller until they gradually disappear. All the parapsychologists are looking for some experiment that can be repeated—that you can do again and get the same effect—statistically, even. They run a million rats—no, it's people this time—they do a lot of things and get a certain statistical effect. Next time they try it they don't get it any more. And now you find a man saying that it is an irrelevant demand to expect a repeatable experiment. This is *science*?

This man also speaks about a new institution, in a talk in which he was resigning as Director of the Institute of Parapsychology. And, in telling people what to do next, he says that one of the things they have to do is be sure they only train students who have shown their ability to get PSI results to an acceptable extent—not to waste their time on those ambitious and interested students who get only chance results. It is very dangerous to have such a policy in teaching—to teach students only how to get certain results, rather than how to do an experiment with scientific integrity.

So I wish to you—I have no more time, so I have just one wish for you—the good luck to be somewhere where you are free to maintain the kind of integrity I have described, and where you do not feel forced by a need to maintain your position in the organization, or financial support, or so on, to lose your integrity. May you have that freedom. May I also give you one last bit of advice: Never say that you'll give a talk unless you know clearly what you're going to talk about and more or less what you're going to say.

Source:
https://calteches.library.caltech.edu/51/2/CargoCult.htm

VR NOTES 5

Virtual Philosophy

Professor Lane's Course Using VR Technology

ASSIGNMENT MODULE SIX | THE SIMULATION HYPOTHESIS

WALTZ OF THE WIZARD APPLICATION

INSTRUCTIONS: After closely reading the following essay about the simulation hypothesis, then enter the Waltz of the Wizard app on your VR headset. It is wondrous and magical place where you can cast spells, interact with all sorts of embedded devices, and even enter into a whole new portal. If you look closely at any one of the objects that you can hold, it will appear very life-like. Now imagine what VR technology will look like in 1,000 years hence, if computational software and hardware keep progressing. Here is the philosophical question I want you to explore, even as you are playing the game: How can do differentiate reality from illusion? Why does magic continually confuse and trick us? Write a 300-word essay on any incident in your life where you took something to be "real" and it turned out to be fake (and/or vice versa)? How did you eventually resolve the conundrum? Place your finished product on your website and be to share your story with other classmates.

THE SIMULATION ARGUMENT:

Why the Probability That You Are Living in a Matrix is Quite High

Nick Bostrom

Times Higher Education Supplement, May 16, 2003

This is a popular piece summarizing Bostrom's academic article: Bostrom, Nick (2003). "Are We Living in a Computer Simulation?" Philosophical Quarterly 53(211). The Matrix got many otherwise not-so-philosophical minds ruminating on the nature of reality. But the scenario depicted in the movie is ridiculous: human brains being kept in tanks by intelligent machines just to produce power. There is, however, a related scenario that is more plausible and a serious line of reasoning that leads from the possibility of this scenario to a striking conclusion about the world we live in. I call this the simulation argument. Perhaps its most startling lesson is that there is a significant probability that you are living in computer simulation. I mean this literally: if the simulation hypothesis is true, you exist in a virtual reality simulated in a computer built by some advanced civilisation. Your brain, too, is merely a part of that simulation. What grounds could we have for taking this hypothesis seriously? Before getting to the gist of the simulation argument, let us consider some of its preliminaries. One of these is the assumption of "substrate independence". This is the idea that conscious minds could in principle be implemented not only on carbon-based biological neurons (such as those inside your head) but also on some other computational substrate such as silicon-based processors. Of course, the computers we have today are not powerful enough to run the computational processes that take place in your brain. Even if they were, we wouldn't know how to program them to do it. But ultimately, what allows you to have conscious experiences is not the fact that your brain is made of squishy, biological matter but rather that it implements a certain computational architecture. This assumption is quite widely (although not universally) accepted among cognitive scientists and philosophers of mind. For the purposes of this article, we shall take it for granted. Given substrate independence, it is in principle possible to implement a human mind on a sufficiently fast computer. Doing so would require very powerful hardware that we do not yet have. It would also require advanced programming abilities, or sophisticated ways of making a very detailed scan of a human brain 2 that could then be uploaded to the computer. Although we will not be able to do this in the near future, the difficulty appears to be merely technical. There is no known physical law or material constraint that would prevent a sufficiently technologically advanced civilisation from implementing human minds in computers. Our second preliminary is that we can estimate, at least roughly, how much computing power it would take to implement a human mind along with a virtual reality that would seem completely realistic for it to interact with. Furthermore, we can establish lower bounds on how powerful the computers of an advanced civilisation could be. Technological futurists have already produced designs for physically possible computers that could be built using advanced molecular manufacturing technology. The upshot of such an analysis is that a technologically mature civilisation that has developed at least those technologies that we already know are physically possible would be able to build computers powerful enough to run an astronomical number of human-like minds, even if only a tiny fraction of their resources was used for that purpose. If you are such a simulated mind, there might be no direct observational way for you to tell; the virtual reality that you would be living in would look and feel perfectly real. But all that this shows, so far, is that you could never be completely sure that you are not living in a simulation. This result is only moderately interesting. You could still regard the simulation hypothesis as too improbable to be taken seriously. Now we get to the core of the simulation argument. This does not purport to demonstrate that you are in a simulation. Instead, it shows that we should accept as true at least one of the following three propositions: (1) The chances that a species at our current level of development can avoid going extinct before becoming technologically mature is negligibly small. (2) Almost no technologically mature civilisations are interested in running computer simulations of minds like ours. (3) You are almost certainly in a simulation. Each of these three propositions may be prima facie implausible; yet, if the simulation argument is correct, at least one is true (it does not tell us which). 3 While the full simulation argument employs some probability theory and formalism, the gist of it can be understood in intuitive terms. Suppose that proposition (1) is false. Then a significant fraction of all species at our level of development eventually becomes technologically mature. Suppose, further, that (2) is false, too. Then some significant fraction of these species that have become technologically mature will use some portion of their computational resources to run computer simulations of minds like ours. But, as we saw earlier, the number of simulated minds that any such technologically mature civilisation could run is astronomically huge. Therefore, if both (1) and (2) are false, there will be an astronomically huge number of simulated minds like ours.

If we work out the numbers, we find that there would be vastly many more such simulated minds than there would be non-simulated minds running on organic brains. In other words, almost all minds like yours, having the kinds of experiences that you have, would be simulated rather than biological. Therefore, by a very weak principle of indifference, you would have to think that you are probably one of these simulated minds rather than one of the exceptional ones that are running on biological neurons. So if you think that (1) and (2) are both false, you should accept (3). It is not coherent to reject all three propositions. In reality, we do not have much specific information to tell us which of the three propositions might be true. In this situation, it might be reasonable to distribute our credence roughly evenly between the three possibilities, giving each of them a substantial probability. Let us consider the options in a little more detail. Possibility (1) is relatively straightforward. For example, maybe there is some highly dangerous technology that every sufficiently advanced civilization develops, and which then destroys them. Let us hope that this is not the case. Possibility (2) requires that there is a strong convergence among all sufficiently advanced civilisations: almost none of them is interested in running computer simulations of minds like ours, and almost none of them contains any relatively wealthy individuals who are interested in doing that and are free to act on their desires. One can imagine various reasons that may lead some civilisations to forgo running simulations, but for (2) to obtain, virtually all civilisations would have to do that. If this were true, it would constitute an interesting constraint on the future evolution of advanced intelligent life. 4 The third possibility is the philosophically most intriguing. If (3) is correct, you are almost certainly now living in computer simulation that was created by some advanced civilisation. What kind of empirical implications would this have? How should it change the way you live your life? Your first reaction might think that if (3) is true, then all bets are off, and that one would go crazy if one seriously thought that one was living in a simulation. To reason thus would be an error. Even if we were in a simulation, the best way to predict what would happen next in our simulation is still the ordinary methods – extrapolation of past trends, scientific modelling, common sense and so on. To a first approximation, if you thought you were in a simulation, you should get on with your life in much the same way as if you were convinced that you are living a nonsimulated life at the bottom level of reality. The simulation hypothesis, however, may have some subtle effects on rational everyday behaviour. To the extent that you think that you understand the motives of the simulators, you can use that understanding to predict what will happen in the simulated world they created. If you think that there is a chance that the simulator of this world happens to be, say, a true-to-faith descendant of some contemporary Christian fundamentalist, you might conjecture that he or she has set up the simulation in such a way that the simulated beings will be rewarded or punished according to Christian moral criteria. An afterlife would, of course, be a real possibility for a simulated creature (who could either be continued in a different simulation after her death or even be "uploaded" into the simulator's universe and perhaps be provided with an artificial body there). Your fate in that afterlife could be made to depend on how you behaved in your present simulated incarnation. Other possible reasons for running simulations include the artistic, scientific or recreational. In the absence of grounds for expecting one kind of simulation rather than another, however, we have to fall back on the ordinary empirical methods for getting about in the world.

If we are in a simulation, is it possible that we could know that for certain? If the simulators don't want us to find out, we probably never will. But if they choose to reveal themselves, they could certainly do so. Maybe a window informing you of the fact would pop up in front of you, or maybe they would "upload" you into their world. Another event that would let us conclude with a very high degree of confidence that we are in a simulation is if we ever reach the point where we are about to switch on our own simulations. If we start running simulations, that would be very strong evidence against (1) and (2). That would leave us with only (3).

VR NOTES 6

Virtual Philosophy

Professor Lane's Course Using VR Technology

ASSIGNMENT MODULE SEVEN | POLITICAL PHILOSOPHY

LITTLE CITIES VR APPLICATION

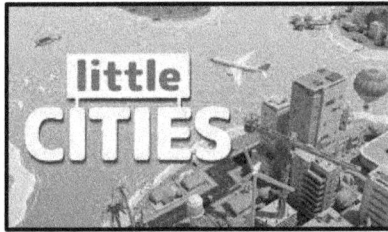

INSTRUCTIONS: After closely reading the following two essays from Adam Smith and Karl Marx reflect on the ideas that each present concerning the formation of ideal governments and their respective political theories that they propound. Using the Little Cities VR application, create your own "ideal" city and test out how best to manage such a large urban population. Be sure to keep a record of what works and what doesn't. What lessons did you learn that were not at first obvious? How did you manage your city's budget, police force, population, building density, parks, etc.? Feel free to experiment with different versions by trial and error. At the end of your experiments, write a 500-word analysis of what you learned and post the same on your website.

THE WEALTH OF NATIONS | ADAM SMITH | BRITANNICA

Despite its renown as the first great work in political economy, The Wealth of Nations is in fact a continuation of the philosophical theme begun in The Theory of Moral Sentiments. The ultimate problem to which Smith addresses himself is how the inner struggle between the passions and the "impartial spectator"—explicated in Moral Sentiments in terms of the single individual—works its effects in the larger arena of history itself, both in the long-run evolution of society and in terms of the immediate characteristics of the stage of history typical of Smith's own day.

Adam Smith

The answer to this problem enters in Book V, in which Smith outlines the four main stages of organization through which society is impelled, unless blocked by wars, deficiencies of resources, or bad policies of government: the original "rude" state of hunters; a second stage of nomadic agriculture; a third stage of feudal, or manorial, "farming"; and a fourth and final stage of commercial interdependence.

It should be noted that each of these stages is accompanied by institutions suited to its needs. For example, in the age of hunters, "there is scarce any property...; so there is seldom any established magistrate or any regular administration of justice." With the advent of flocks there emerges a more complex form of social organization, comprising not only "formidable" armies but the central institution of private property with its indispensable buttress of law and order as well. It is the very essence of Smith's thought that he recognized this institution, whose social usefulness he never doubted, as an instrument for the protection of privilege, rather than one to be justified in terms of natural law: "Civil government," he wrote, "so far as it is instituted for the security of property, is in reality instituted for the defence of the rich against the poor, or of those who have some property against those who have none at all." Finally, Smith describes the evolution through feudalism into a stage of society requiring new institutions, such as market-determined rather than guild-determined wages and free rather than government-constrained enterprise. This later became known as laissez-faire capitalism; Smith called it the system of perfect liberty.

There is an obvious resemblance between this succession of changes in the material basis of production, each bringing its requisite alterations in the superstructure of laws and civil institutions, and the Marxian conception of history. Though the resemblance is indeed remarkable, there is also a crucial difference: in the Marxian scheme the engine of evolution is ultimately the struggle between contending classes, whereas in Smith's philosophical history the primal moving agency is "human nature" driven by the desire for self-betterment and guided (or misguided) by the faculties of reason.

Society and the "invisible hand"

The theory of historical evolution, although it is perhaps the binding conception of The Wealth of Nations, is subordinated within the work itself to a detailed description of how the "invisible hand" actually operates within the commercial, or final, stage of society. This becomes the focus of Books I and II, in which Smith undertakes to elucidate two questions. The first is how a system of perfect liberty, operating under the drives and constraints of human nature and intelligently designed institutions, will give rise to an orderly society. The question, which had already been considerably elucidated by earlier writers, required both an explanation of the underlying orderliness in the pricing of individual commodities and an explanation of the "laws" that regulated the division of the entire "wealth" of the nation (which Smith saw as its annual production of goods and services) among the three great claimant classes— labourers, landlords, and manufacturers.

This orderliness, as would be expected, was produced by the interaction of the two aspects of human nature: its response to its passions and its susceptibility to reason and sympathy. But whereas The Theory of Moral Sentiments had relied mainly on the presence of the "inner man" to provide the necessary restraints to private action, in The Wealth of Nations one finds an institutional mechanism that acts to reconcile the disruptive possibilities inherent in a blind obedience to the passions alone. This protective mechanism is competition, an arrangement by which the passionate desire for bettering one's condition—"a desire that comes with us from the womb, and never leaves us until we go into the grave"—is turned into a socially beneficial agency by pitting one person's drive for self-betterment against another's.

It is in the unintended outcome of this competitive struggle for self-betterment that the invisible hand regulating the economy shows itself, for Smith explains how mutual vying forces the prices of commodities down to their "natural" levels, which correspond to their costs of production. Moreover, by inducing labour and capital to move from less to more profitable occupations or areas, the competitive mechanism constantly restores prices to these "natural" levels despite short-run aberrations. Finally, by explaining that wages and rents and profits (the constituent parts of the costs of production) are themselves subject to this same discipline of self-interest and competition, Smith not only provided an ultimate rationale for these "natural" prices but also revealed an underlying orderliness in the distribution of income itself among workers, whose recompense was their wages; landlords, whose income was their rents; and manufacturers, whose reward was their profits.

Economic growth

Smith's analysis of the market as a self-correcting mechanism was impressive. But his purpose was more ambitious than to demonstrate the self-adjusting properties of the system. Rather, it was to show that, under the impetus of the acquisitive drive, the annual flow of national wealth could be seen to grow steadily.

Smith's explanation of economic growth, although not neatly assembled in one part of The Wealth of Nations, is quite clear. The core of it lies in his emphasis on the division of labour (itself an outgrowth of the "natural" propensity to trade) as the source of society's capacity to increase its productivity. The Wealth of Nations opens with a famous passage describing a pin factory in which 10 persons, by specializing in various tasks, turn out 48,000 pins a day, compared with the few pins, perhaps only 1, that each could have produced alone. But this all-important division of labour does not take place unaided. It can occur only after the prior accumulation of capital (or stock, as Smith calls it), which is used to pay the additional workers and to buy tools and machines.

The drive for accumulation, however, brings problems. The manufacturer who accumulates stock needs more labourers (since labour-saving technology has no place in Smith's scheme), and, in attempting to hire them, he bids up their wages above their "natural" price. Consequently, his profits begin to fall, and the process of accumulation is in danger of ceasing. But now there enters an ingenious mechanism for continuing the advance: in bidding up the price of labour, the manufacturer inadvertently sets into motion a process that increases the supply of labour, for "the demand for men, like that for any other commodity, necessarily regulates the production of men." Specifically, Smith had in mind the effect of higher wages in lessening child mortality. Under the influence of a larger labour supply, the wage rise is moderated and profits are maintained; the new supply of labourers offers a continuing opportunity for the manufacturer to introduce a further division of labour and thereby add to the system's growth.

Here then was a "machine" for growth—a machine that operated with all the reliability of the Newtonian system with which Smith was quite familiar. Unlike the Newtonian system, however, Smith's growth machine did not depend for its operation on the laws of nature alone. Human nature drove it, and human nature was a complex rather than a simple force. Thus, the wealth of nations would grow only if individuals, through their governments, did not inhibit this growth by catering to the pleas for special privilege that would prevent the competitive system from exerting its benign effect. Consequently, much of The Wealth of Nations, especially Book IV, is a polemic against the restrictive measures of the "mercantile system" that favoured monopolies at home and abroad. Smith's system of "natural liberty," he is careful to point out, accords with the best interests of all but will not be put into practice if government is entrusted to, or heeds, "the mean rapacity, the monopolizing spirit of merchants and manufacturers, who neither are, nor ought to be, the rulers of mankind."

The Wealth of Nations is therefore far from the ideological tract it is often assumed to be. Although Smith preached laissez-faire (with important exceptions), his argument was directed as much against monopoly as against government; and although he extolled the social results of the acquisitive process, he almost invariably treated the manners and maneuvers of businessmen with contempt. Nor did he see the commercial system itself as wholly admirable. He wrote with discernment about the intellectual degradation of the worker in a society in which the division of labour has proceeded very far; by comparison with the alert intelligence of the husbandman, the specialized worker "generally becomes as stupid and ignorant as it is possible for a human being to become."

In all of this, it is notable that Smith was writing in an age of preindustrial capitalism. He seems to have had no real presentiment of the gathering Industrial Revolution, harbingers of which were visible in the great ironworks only a few miles from Edinburgh. He had nothing to say about large-scale industrial enterprise, and the few remarks in The Wealth of Nations concerning the future of joint-stock companies (corporations) are disparaging. Finally, one should bear in mind that, if growth is the great theme of The Wealth of Nations, it is not unending growth. Here and there in the treatise are glimpses of a secularly declining rate of profit; and Smith mentions as well the prospect that when the system eventually accumulates its "full complement of riches"—all the pin factories, so to speak, whose output could be absorbed—economic decline would begin, ending in an impoverished stagnation.

The Wealth of Nations was received with admiration by Smith's wide circle of friends and admirers, although it was by no means an immediate popular success. The work finished, Smith went into semiretirement. The year following its publication he was appointed commissioner both of customs and of salt duties for Scotland, posts that brought him £600 a year. He thereupon informed his former charge that he no longer required his pension, to which Buccleuch replied that his sense of honour would never allow him to stop paying it. Smith was therefore quite well off in the final years of his life, which were spent mainly in Edinburgh with occasional trips to London or Glasgow (which appointed him a rector of the university). The years passed quietly, with several revisions of both major books but with no further publications. He died at the age of 67, full of honours and recognition, and was buried in the churchyard at Canongate with a simple monument stating that Adam Smith, author of The Wealth of Nations, lay there.

Legacy of Adam Smith

Beyond the few facts of his life, which can be embroidered only in detail, exasperatingly little is known about the man. Smith never married, and almost nothing is known of his personal side. Moreover, it was the custom of his time to destroy rather than to preserve the private files of illustrious men, with the unhappy result that much of Smith's unfinished work, as well as his personal papers, was destroyed (some as late as 1942). Only one portrait of Smith survives, a profile medallion by James Tassie; it gives a glimpse of the older man with his somewhat heavy-lidded eyes, aquiline nose, and a hint of a protrusive lower lip. "I am a beau in nothing but my books," Smith once told a friend to whom he was showing his library of some 3,000 volumes.

From various accounts, he was also a man of many peculiarities, which included a stumbling manner of speech (until he had warmed to his subject), a gait described as "vermicular," and above all an extraordinary and even comic absence of mind. On the other hand, contemporaries wrote of a smile of "inexpressible benignity" and of his political tact and dispatch in managing the sometimes acerbic business of the Glasgow faculty.

Certainly, he enjoyed a high measure of contemporary fame; even in his early days at Glasgow his reputation attracted students from nations as distant as Russia, and his later years were crowned not only with expressions of admiration from many European thinkers but by a growing recognition among British governing circles that his work provided a rationale of inestimable importance for practical economic policy.

Over the years, Smith's lustre as a social philosopher has escaped much of the weathering that has affected the reputations of other first-rate political economists. Although he was writing for his generation, the breadth of his knowledge, the cutting edge of his generalizations, and the boldness of his vision have never ceased to attract the admiration of all social scientists, economists in particular. Couched in the spacious, cadenced prose of his period, rich in imagery and crowded with life, The Wealth of Nations projects a sanguine but never sentimental image of society.

Never so finely analytic as David Ricardo nor so stern and profound as Karl Marx, Smith is the very epitome of the Enlightenment: hopeful but realistic, speculative but practical, always respectful of the classical past but ultimately dedicated to the great discovery of his age—progress.

Robert L. Heilbroner

Source: https://www.britannica.com/biography/Adam-Smith/The-Wealth-of-Nations

---

HISTORICAL MATERIALISM | KARL MARX | BRITANNICA

In 1859, in the preface to his Zur Kritik der politischen Ökonomie (Contribution to the Critique of Political Economy), Marx wrote that the hypothesis that had served him as the basis for his analysis of society could be briefly formulated as follows:

In the social production that men carry on, they enter into definite relations that are indispensable and independent of their will, relations of production which correspond to a definite stage of development of their material forces of production. The sum total of these relations of production constitutes the economic structure of society, the real foundation, on which rises a legal and political superstructure, and to which correspond definite forms of social consciousness. The mode of production in material life determines the general character of the social, political, and intellectual processes of life. It is not the consciousness of men which determines their existence; it is on the contrary their social existence which determines their consciousness.

Raised to the level of historical law, this hypothesis was subsequently called historical materialism. Marx applied it to capitalist society, both in Manifest der kommunistischen Partei (1848; The Communist Manifesto) and Das Kapital (vol. 1, 1867; "Capital") and in other writings. Although Marx reflected upon his working hypothesis for many years, he did not formulate it in a very exact manner: different expressions served him for identical realities. If one takes the text literally, social reality is structured in the following way:

1. Underlying everything as the real basis of society is the economic structure. This structure includes (a) the "material forces of production," that is, the labour and means of production, and (b) the overall "relations of production," or the social and political arrangements that regulate production and distribution. Although Marx stated that there is a correspondence between the "material forces" of production and the indispensable "relations" of production, he never made himself clear on the nature of the correspondence, a fact that was to be the source of differing interpretations among his later followers.

2. Above the economic structure rises the superstructure, consisting of legal and political "forms of social consciousness" that correspond to the economic structure. Marx says nothing about the nature of this correspondence between ideological forms and economic structure, except that through the ideological forms individuals become conscious of the conflict within the economic structure

between the material forces of production and the existing relations of production expressed in the legal property relations. In other words, "The sum total of the forces of production accessible to men determines the condition of society" and is at the base of society. "The social structure and the state issue continually from the life processes of definite individuals . . . as they are in reality, that is acting and materially producing." The political relations that individuals establish among themselves are dependent on material production, as are the legal relations. This foundation of the social on the economic is not an incidental point: it colours Marx's whole analysis. It is found in Das Kapital as well as in Die deutsche Ideologie (written 1845–46; The German Ideology) and the Ökonomisch-philosophische Manuskripte aus dem Jahre 1844 (Economic and Philosophic Manuscripts of 1844).

Source: https://www.britannica.com/topic/Marxism

VR NOTES 7

Virtual Philosophy

Professor Lane's Course Using VR Technology

ASSIGNMENT MODULE EIGHT | THE UNIVERSE

SPHERES VR APPLICATION

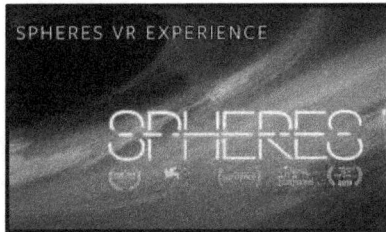

INSTRUCTIONS: After reading the timeline about the history of our universe and the essay about the multiverse sit back and watch the immersive Spheres VR. When finished write down your own autobiographical reaction to what you have experienced, responding to the following three questions: 1) How do you feel knowing how immensely large the universe is? 2) What do you find most intriguing about the cosmos at large? 3) What questions would you like to see answered about our life here on terra firma (e.g., Is there life on other planets?). In addition, answer the following query: why is understanding physics and astronomy important for doing philosophy? Be sure to do some further research to best answer this question. Post your responses on your website and share with your classmates.

Universe Timeline | Nova Online | Alpha to Omega

The Big Bang

0.0000000000000000000000000000000000001 seconds after the Big Bang

The universe began with a vast explosion that generated space and time, and created all the matter and energy in the universe. Exactly what triggered this sudden expansion remains a mystery. Astronomers believe it involved a runaway process called "inflation," in which a peculiar type of energy that existed in the vacuum of space was suddenly mobilized. The inflationary expansion ended only when this energy was transformed into more familiar forms of matter and energy.

1 second after the big bang

After inflation ended in the first tiny fraction of a second, the universe continued to expand but not nearly so quickly. As the universe cooled, the most basic forces in nature emerged: first gravity, then the strong force, which holds nuclei of atoms together, followed by the weak and electromagnetic forces. In its first second of existence, the universe was made up of fundamental particles, including quarks, electrons, photons, and neutrinos. Protons and neutrons then began to form.

Basic Elements Form

3 minutes after the big bang

In the next few minutes, the universe as we know it took shape. Already incomprehensibly large, its protons and neutrons came together to form the nuclei of simple elements. That the universe remains largely made up of these elements—hydrogen and helium—is considered strong evidence of the validity of the big bang model.

From Hot to Cold

500,000 years after the big bang

For the next 300,000 to 500,000 years or so, the universe remained an enormous cloud of hot expanding gas. When this gas had cooled to a critical threshold, electrons were able to combine with hydrogen and helium nuclei. Photons no longer scattered, but rushed outward. We can still see the photons emitted from this period, but time and distance have shifted them into microwave wavelengths. Today, this cosmic microwave background radiation gives astronomers a window onto the early universe.

Birth of Stars and Galaxies

1,000,000,000 years after the big bang

As time moved forward, the pull of gravity exerted its influence on the early universe. It amplified slight irregularities in the density of the primordial gas. Even as the universe as a whole continued to expand, pockets of gas became more and more dense. Stars ignited within these pockets. Groups of stars then became the earliest galaxies. Modern telescopes can detect these primordial galaxies as they appeared when the universe was only one billion years old, just 7 percent of its present age.

The Era of Quasars

3,000,000,000 years after the big bang

From one billion to three billion years after the big bang many smaller galaxies merged into larger ones, forming an array of shapes resembling spirals and spheres (known as elliptical galaxies). Often the merger was so violent that stars and gas collapsed into a common center, becoming so dense they formed gigantic black holes. The gas flowing into these black holes became hot enough to glow brightly before it disappeared. The light of these "quasars" can be seen across the depths of the universe.

Supernova 9933

6,000,000,000 years after the big bang

Within galaxies, as stars were being born, others died...often in enormous cataclysmic explosions. These explosions, called supernovae, are important to the evolution of galaxies because they distribute all the common elements such as oxygen, carbon, nitrogen, calcium, and iron into interstellar space. Explosions of especially massive stars also create and distribute heavier elements such as gold, silver, lead, and uranium. The supernova pictured here is of a smaller type, used by astronomers to determine distance. This one appears to us now as it looked when the universe was about five billion years old.

Birth of the Sun

5,000,000,000 years before the present

The sun formed within a cloud of gas in a spiral arm of the Milky Way galaxy. A vast disk of gas and debris that swirled around this new star coalesced into planets, moons, and asteroids.

The image on the left, from the Hubble Space Telescope, shows a star in the throes of birth. Powerful jets of radiation roar out of its poles, lighting up the surrounding environment.

Galaxies Collide

3,000,000,000 years in the future

Astronomers estimate that in about three billion years, our Milky Way galaxy will be swallowed up by one of its nearest neighbors, a large galaxy named Andromeda that lies 2.2 million light-years away. Depending on their pathways, these two galaxies will either merge into a single gigantic galaxy or rip each other apart, sending millions of stars like our sun hurling into space. One such titanic collision involving four galaxies, 300 million light-years away, is pictured at left.

Galaxies Disappear

100,000,000,000 years in the future

If recent observations of cosmic acceleration are correct, then the "vacuum energy" that is emerging in the universe will continue to overtake the pull of gravity from matter. This means that, in the future, gravitationally bound clusters of galaxies will survive but galaxies in general will fly ever more rapidly apart. Eventually our nearest unbound neighbors will be so far away that they will no longer be seen, even with big telescopes. But this will be so far in the future that our sun will have long since burned out and our Earth died with it.

Stellar Era Ends

1,000,000,000,000 years in the future

During this era, which will last from 100 billion years to one trillion years after the big bang (and is the era we are currently in), most of the energy generated by the universe will be in the form of stars burning hydrogen and other elements in their cores. This long period will give way to an even longer, lingering death for our universe.

The Degenerate Era

10,000,000,000,000,000,000,000,000,000,000,000,000 years in the future

This era extends to ten trillion trillion trillion years after the big bang. Most of the mass that we can currently see in the universe will be contained in stars that have blown up and collapsed into black holes and neutron stars. Or it will be locked up in brown dwarfs and planets that never triggered nuclear fusion, or in stars that withered into white dwarfs. With stars no longer actively burning, energy in this era is generated through proton decay and particle annihilation.

The Black Hole Era

**10,000,000,000,000,000,000,000,000,000,000,000,
000,000,000,000,000,000,000,000,000,000,00
0,000,000,000,000,000,000,000,000 years in the future**

This era extends to ten thousand trillion trillion trillion trillion trillion trillion trillion trillion years after the big bang. After the epoch of proton decay, the only star-like objects remaining are black holes of widely varying masses. Their energy is steadily evaporating.

The Dark Era

**>10,000,000,000,000,000,000,000,000,000,000,000
,000,000,000,000,000,000,000,000,000,000,000,00
0,000,000,000,000,000,000,000,000 years in the future**

At this late stage, protons will have decayed and black holes will have almost completely evaporated. Only the byproducts of these processes remain: mostly neutrinos, electrons, positrons, and photons of enormous wavelengths. For all intents and purposes, the universe as we know it will have come to an end.

SOURCE:
https://www.pbs.org/wgbh/nova/universe/historywave.html

IS THE UNIVERSE REALLY MADE OUT OF TINY RUBBER BANDS?

A Kid's Exploration of String Theory

Hi, my name is Shaun. However, my parents' pet name for me is Plato. I have always wondered about the origin of matter. Once I took an old golf ball and broke it apart. I was surprised to see that there were tightly woven rubber bands inside.

This got me to thinking about what made up rubber bands. So, I went to my father and mother and they suggested that I look into the subject of physics, but more specifically into the subject of quantum mechanics, which is the study of how very small things behave.

Richard Feynman, a very famous scientist who worked on developing the first atom bomb, was once asked if he could try to explain all of physics in one simple sentence. His reply was pretty funny, but quite profound: "Things are made of littler things that jiggle."

"So if this was true," I thought to myself, "then I could unlock the secret of matter by breaking things down to their smaller parts and seeing how they moved around."

When I took apart a rubber band I found out they were made of even smaller lines of rubber. But when I went and pulled those apart all I got were little pieces.

I couldn't go any farther with my bare hands so I got my microscope out and when I got the piece positioned just right I could see that it was made of smaller thread like material.

"What is that stuff?" I pondered.

My microscope was pretty limited so I couldn't break the rubber down much farther. I was stuck in a sort cul du sac, similar to the street I live on which has a dead end to it.

What to do?

I then realized I had to learn from the great physicists in the past who have explored this subject in depth.

This is when I learned about the early Greek philosopher, Democritus, who suggested that all things are made up of little tiny balls which he called atoms which he thought were uncuttable. This turned out later to be wrong since atoms can be broken apart, but the word atoms became a popular way of talking about really tiny things.

In the 19th and 20th century, physicists realized that atoms were comprised of mostly empty space. But in their core was a seed like thing called a nucleus which houses smaller bits of matter called protons and neutrons. And darting around that nucleus seed was a superfast particle called an electron.

I found it intriguing that the number of protons and electrons in an atom are recognized as different chemical elements such as hydrogen (the simplest atom with only one proton and one electron) and uranium (an atom with 92 protons and 92 electrons). These different atomic numbers explain why some things are solid and dense, such as gold, and other things are airy and flighty such as when you put helium in a balloon.

Everything we see around us is just the mixing of different types of atoms.

Yet, this got me to look further into the heart of atoms. What is inside protons and neutrons? What is light?

Scientists such as Max Planck, Albert Einstein, Niels Bohr, Max Born, Erwin Schrodinger, Paul Dirac, Wolfgang Pauli, and Werner Heisenberg developed a new way of understanding physics which became popularly known as quantum mechanics. Just as an auto mechanic tries to understand what is wrong with your car by opening up the hood and looking closely at the car's engine, the quantum mechanic looks under the hood of the atom to see how the tiny bits of matter are working together.

Physicists were shocked to realize that matter at very small scales behaves in completely unexpected ways. Indeed the more they tried to figure out the exact location and speed of an electron, they noticed that their very act of trying to measure both interfered with the electron. Thus, scientists couldn't know both precisely.

Imagine that you are rolling a pair of dice outside in the dark and you couldn't see what numbers you rolled.

However, when you put your flashlight on the dice, the light itself changed the roll of the dice so that you couldn't know what your original throw was.

Your very act of shining light on the dice literally altered your throw. This is very similar to what happens when physicists try to figure out what electrons are really doing only to realize that their very act of observing changed what they observed.

This understanding caused a revolution in physics and started them on a new course where chance and probability played an important part in studying the secrets of nature.

They realized that there were four fundamental forces in the universe: 1. Electromagnetism (which is where we get light and electricity and our food from); 2. Strong nuclear force (this keeps protons and neutrons bonded together for the most part); 3). Weak nuclear force (which explains why there is radioactive decay within atoms). 4. Gravity (which is the universal attractive force which explains why the earth orbits the sun and why I cannot jump very high when I play basketball).

But scientists wondered if all four of these forces were the result of one very tiny super process. They called this quest a G.U.T, which stands for Grand Unified Theory or a T.O.E., a Theory of Everything. This made me laugh thinking that the hidden mystery of the universe was in a TOE or a GUT.

Scientists realized that to find out the hidden parts of atoms they had to investigate even smaller bits. In order to do this they had to force protons to break apart so they could see what they contained. So scientists built big colliders where they had protons zipping around near the speed of light in large circular tracks until they hit each other and broke apart.

This reminded me of when I would occasionally take a shell or a rock at the beach and try to open it apart and see what is inside of it. The secret of the universe is in the tiniest bits of matter. In the 1980s a new theory was developed called String theory which essentially claims that everything in the universe is made out of very small loops of matter, much, much smaller than anything we can see in atoms. These strings vibrate in various ways and thus cause various forms of matter to be created.

All the elementary particles that make up our universe are like musical notes which are caused by infinitesimally small loops of guitar like string (sometimes open and sometimes closed). Strike a different vibration of one of these strings and a different physical property emerges.

These strings, however, are so small that nobody can see them, not even with the world's most powerful microscope.

This is why scientists built a Large Hadron Collider in Switzerland which is pretty deep underground so they could smash protons against each other and try to recreate the initial conditions shortly after the Big Bang. The Big Bang is when our universe started 13.7 billion years ago.

Everything back then was collapsed into a tiny little seed, including all the stars and the planets. This single point was much smaller than a penny but it was amazingly heavy with all that packed in energy and matter. So when it exploded it was called a "Big Bang."

In this way scientists realized that if they could understand the very small they could also unlock the secrets of the very large, since at the beginning of time everything came from the tiniest of seeds.

One of the most interesting aspects of string theory is that there may be many more dimensions than we presently see. We know of four dimensions: length, width, depth, and time. But string theory says there may be 11 dimensions which are curled up so small that we cannot access them.

I couldn't visualize this at all, but Brian Greene, the famous Professor of Physics at Columbia University, in a film series gave a good illustration of it. He pointed to a lawn and said that if you were an ant the blades of grass would seem like trees, but if you were up in an airplane looking down at that same lawn it would flat and dimensionless.

One of the coolest ideas being suggested by science is that the universe we live in may be only one of trillions of other universes. They have called this the multiverse.

Apparently, all of these universes may result from slight changes in the vibrations of extraordinarily tiny strings of energy/matter, just as a few chord changes can produce a new song. The problem with string theory is that it hasn't yet been proven by science. However, scientists have proposed a number of experiments, including some connected to the Large Hadron Collider, which will be able to demonstrate whether string theory is true or not. Because string theory is open to being tested it is not simply philosophy or wishful thinking.

I never realized that a simple golf ball when broken down could be so complex when it is viewed from smaller and smaller scales.

My dad suggested that a quote from the poet Tennyson actually summarizes my project perfectly, "if we could but understand a single flower we would know who we are and what the world is."

I found it amusing when I thought of how my golf ball was made of smaller rubber bands which when squished up appeared solid. This got me to thinking about string theory in a different way: maybe the universe, like my golf ball, is really just made of tiny rubber bands that we cannot see! Or, maybe I am also a unique strand of strings.

NOTES

I had a lot of fun doing this project. I learned the most from watching Brian Greene's two NOVA specials (which are several hours each), The Elegant Universe and The Fabric of the Cosmos. I also recommend reading Quantum Physics by John Gribbin. If you want to have a short introduction to the subject of String Theory, I recommend Professor Greene's recent T.E.D. talk "Is Our Universe the Only Universe?"

SOURCE: https://www.integralworld.net/diem-lane10.html

VR NOTES 8

Virtual Philosophy

Professor Lane's Course Using VR Technology

ASSIGNMENT MODULE NINE | EXISTENTIALISM

PAPER BIRDS APPLICATION

INSTRUCTIONS: Watch the two-part series, Paper Birds, paying close attention to the mood and plot of the interactive film and how the main character finds meaning. After this read the following short stories about seeking meaning and purpose. Now create your own fictional story, replete with a chief character of your own invention, who confronts a crisis of meaning in his/her own life. How do they ultimately resolve their crisis? Be as creative as possible. Post your fictional story on your website and share it with your classmates. Word length: 250 words minimum and the sky is the limit.

THE COFFEE HOUSE OF SURAT | Leo Tolstoy

In the town of Surat, in India, was a coffee-house where many travelers and foreigners from all parts of the world met and conversed.

One day a learned Persian theologian visited this coffee-house. He was a man who had spent his life studying the nature of the Deity, and reading and writing books upon the subject. He had thought, read, and written so much about God, that eventually he lost his wits, became quite confused, and ceased even to believe in the existence of a God. The Shah, hearing of this, had banished him from Persia.

After having argued all his life about the First Cause, this unfortunate theologian had ended by quite perplexing himself, and instead of understanding that he had lost his own reason, he began to think that there was no higher Reason controlling the universe.

This man had an African slave who followed him everywhere. When the theologian entered the coffee-house, the slave remained outside, near the door, sitting on a stone in the glare of the sun, and driving away the flies that buzzed around him. The Persian having settled down on a divan in the coffee-house, ordered himself a cup of opium. When he had drunk it and the opium had begun to quicken the workings of his brain, he addressed his slave through the open door:

'Tell me, wretched slave,' said he, 'do you think there is a God, or not?'

'Of course there is,' said the slave, and immediately drew from under his girdle a small idol of wood.

'There,' said he, 'that is the God who has guarded me from the day of my birth. Every one in our country worships the fetish tree, from the wood of which this God was made.'

This conversation between the theologian and his slave was listened to with surprise by the other guests in the coffee-house. They were astonished at the master's question, and yet more so at the slave's reply.

One of them, a Brahmin, on hearing the words spoken by the slave, turned to him and said:

'Miserable fool! Is it possible you believe that God can be carried under a man's girdle? There is one God—Brahma, and he is greater than the whole world, for he created it. Brahma is the One, the mighty God, and in His honor are built the temples on the Ganges' banks, where his true priests, the Brahmins, worship him. They know the true God, and none but they. A thousand score of years have passed, and yet through revolution after revolution these priests have held their sway, because Brahma, the one true God, has protected them.'

So spoke the Brahmin, thinking to convince every one; but a Jewish broker who was present replied to him, and said:

'No! the temple of the true God is not in India. Neither does God protect the Brahmin caste. The true God is not the God of the Brahmins, but of Abraham, Isaac, and Jacob. None does He protect but His chosen people, the Israelites. From the commencement of the world, our nation has been beloved of Him, and ours alone. If we are now scattered over the whole earth, it is but to try us; for God has promised that He will one day gather His people together in Jerusalem. Then, with the Temple of Jerusalem—the wonder of the ancient world—restored to its splendor, shall Israel be established a ruler over all nations.'

So spoke the Jew, and burst into tears. He wished to say more, but an Italian missionary who was there interrupted him.

'What you are saying is untrue,' said he to the Jew. 'You attribute injustice to God. He cannot love your nation above the rest. Nay rather, even if it be true that of old He favored the Israelites, it is now nineteen hundred years since they angered Him, and caused Him to destroy their nation and scatter them over the earth, so that their faith makes no converts and has died out except here and there. God shows preference to no nation, but calls all who wish to be saved to the bosom of the Catholic Church of Rome, the one outside whose borders no salvation can be found.'

So spoke the Italian. But a Protestant minister, who happened to be present, growing pale, turned to the Catholic missionary and exclaimed:

'How can you say that salvation belongs to your religion? Those only will be saved, who serve God according to the Gospel, in spirit and in truth, as bidden by the word of Christ.'

Then a Turk, an office-holder in the custom-house at Surat, who was sitting in the coffee-house smoking a pipe, turned with an air of superiority to both the Christians.

'Your belief in your Roman religion is vain,' said he. 'It was superseded twelve hundred years ago by the true faith: that of Mohammed! You cannot but observe how the true Mohammedan faith continues to spread both in Europe and Asia, and even in the enlightened country of China. You say yourselves that God has rejected the Jews; and, as a proof, you quote the fact that the Jews are humiliated and their faith does not spread. Confess then the truth of Mohammedanism, for it is triumphant and spreads far and wide. None will be saved but the followers of Mohammed, God's latest prophet; and of them, only the followers of Omar, and not of Ali, for the latter are false to the faith.'

To this the Persian theologian, who was of the sect of Ali, wished to reply; but by this time a great dispute had arisen among all the strangers of different faiths and creeds present. There were Abyssinian Christians, Llamas from Thibet, Ismailians and Fireworshippers. They all argued about the nature of God, and how He should be worshiped. Each of them asserted that in his country alone was the true God known and rightly worshiped.

Every one argued and shouted, except a Chinaman, a student of Confucius, who sat quietly in one corner of the coffee-house, not joining in the dispute. He sat there drinking tea and listening to what the others said, but did not speak himself.

The Turk noticed him sitting there, and appealed to him, saying:

'You can confirm what I say, my good Chinaman. You hold your peace, but if you spoke I know you would uphold my opinion. Traders from your country, who come to me for assistance, tell me that though many religions have been introduced into China, you Chinese consider Mohammedanism the best of all, and adopt it willingly. Confirm, then, my words, and tell us your opinion of the true God and of His prophet.'

'Yes, yes,' said the rest, turning to the Chinaman, 'let us hear what you think on the subject.'

The Chinaman, the student of Confucius, closed his eyes, and thought a while. Then he opened them again, and drawing his hands out of the wide sleeves of his garment, and folding them on his breast, he spoke as follows, in a calm and quiet voice.

Sirs, it seems to me that it is chiefly pride that prevents men agreeing with one another on matters of faith. If you care to listen to me, I will tell you a story which will explain this by an example.

I came here from China on an English steamer which had been round the world. We stopped for fresh water, and landed on the east coast of the island of Sumatra. It was mid-day, and some of us, having landed, sat in the shade of some coconut palms by the seashore, not far from a native village. We were a party of men of different nationalities.

As we sat there, a blind man approached us. We learned afterwards that he had gone blind from gazing too long and too persistently at the sun, trying to find out what it is, in order to seize its light.

He strove a long time to accomplish this, constantly looking at the sun; but the only result was that his eyes were injured by its brightness, and he became blind.

Then he said to himself:

'The light of the sun is not a liquid; for if it were a liquid it would be possible to pour it from one vessel into another, and it would be moved, like water, by the wind. Neither is it fire; for if it were fire, water would extinguish it. Neither is light a spirit, for it is seen by the eye; nor is it matter, for it cannot be moved. Therefore, as the light of the sun is neither liquid, nor fire, nor spirit, nor matter, it is—nothing!'

So he argued, and, as a result of always looking at the sun and always thinking about it, he lost both his sight and his reason. And when he went quite blind, he became fully convinced that the sun did not exist.

With this blind man came a slave, who after placing his master in the shade of a coconut tree, picked up a coconut from the ground, and began making it into a night-light. He twisted a wick from the fiber of the coconut: squeezed oil from the nut into the shell, and soaked the wick in it.

As the slave sat doing this, the blind man sighed and said to him:

'Well, slave, was I not right when I told you there is no sun? Do you not see how dark it is? Yet people say there is a sun. . . . But if so, what is it?'

'I do not know what the sun is,' said the slave. 'That is no business of mine. But I know what light is. Here I have made a night-light, by the help of which I can serve you and find anything I want in the hut.'

And the slave picked up the coconut shell, saying:

'This is my sun.'

A lame man with crutches, who was sitting near by, heard these words, and laughed:

'You have evidently been blind all your life,' said he to the blind man, 'not to know what the sun is. I will tell you what it is. The sun is a ball of fire, which rises every morning out of the sea and goes down again among the mountains of our island each evening. We have all seen this, and if you had had your eyesight you too would have seen it.'

A fisherman, who had been listening to the conversation said:

'It is plain enough that you have never been beyond your own island. If you were not lame, and if you had been out as I have in a fishing-boat, you would know that the sun does not set among the mountains of our island, but as it rises from the ocean every morning so it sets again in the sea every night. What I am telling you is true, for I see it every day with my own eyes.'

Then an Indian who was of our party, interrupted him by saying:

'I am astonished that a reasonable man should talk such nonsense. How can a ball of fire possibly descend into the water and not be extinguished? The sun is not a ball of fire at all, it is the Deity named Deva, who rides for ever in a chariot round the golden mountain, Meru. Sometimes the evil serpents Ragu and Ketu attack Deva and swallow him: and then the earth is dark. But our priests pray that the Deity may be released, and then he is set free. Only such ignorant men as you, who have never been beyond their own island, can imagine that the sun shines for their country alone.'

Then the master of an Egyptian vessel, who was present, spoke in his turn.

'No,' said he, 'you also are wrong. The sun is not a Deity, and does not move only round India and its golden mountain. I have sailed much on the Black Sea, and along the coasts of Arabia, and have been to Madagascar and to the Philippines. The sun lights the whole earth, and not India alone. It does not circle round one mountain, but rises far in the East, beyond the Isles of Japan, and sets far, far away in the West, beyond the islands of England. That is why the Japanese call their country "Nippon," that is, "the birth of the sun." I know this well, for I have myself seen much, and heard more from my grandfather, who sailed to the very ends of the sea.'

He would have gone on, but an English sailor from our ship interrupted him.

'There is no country,' he said, 'where people know so much about the sun's movements as in England. The sun, as every one in England knows, rises nowhere and sets nowhere. It is always moving round the earth. We can be sure of this for we have just been round the world ourselves, and nowhere knocked up against the sun. Wherever we went, the sun showed itself in the morning and hid itself at night, just as it does here.'

And the Englishman took a stick and, drawing circles on the sand, tried to explain how the sun moves in the heavens and goes round the world. But he was unable to explain it clearly, and pointing to the ship's pilot said:

'This man knows more about it than I do. He can explain it properly.'

The pilot, who was an intelligent man, had listened in silence to the talk till he was asked to speak. Now every one turned to him, and he said:

'You are all misleading one another, and are yourselves deceived. The sun does not go round the earth, but the earth goes round the sun, revolving as it goes, and turning towards the sun in the course of each twenty-four hours, not only Japan, and the Philippines, and Sumatra where we now are, but Africa, and Europe, and America, and many lands besides. The sun does not shine for some one mountain, or for some one island, or for some one sea, nor even for one earth alone, but for other planets as well as our earth. If you would only look up at the heavens, instead of at the ground beneath your own feet, you might all understand this, and would then no longer suppose that the sun shines for you, or for your country alone.'

Thus spoke the wise pilot, who had voyaged much about the world, and had gazed much upon the heavens above.

'So on matters of faith,' continued the Chinaman, the student of Confucius, 'it is pride that causes error and discord among men. As with the sun, so it is with God. Each man wants to have a special God of his own, or at least a special God for his native land. Each nation wishes to confine in its own temples Him, whom the world cannot contain.

'Can any temple compare with that which God Himself has built to unite all men in one faith and one religion?

'All human temples are built on the model of this temple, which is God's own world. Every temple has its fonts, its vaulted roof, its lamps, its pictures or sculptures, its inscriptions, its books of the law, its offerings, its altars and its priests. But in what temple is there such a font as the ocean; such a vault as that of the heavens; such lamps as the sun, moon, and stars; or any figures to be compared with living, loving, mutually-helpful men? Where are there any records of God's goodness so easy to understand as the blessings which God has strewn abroad for man's happiness? Where is there any book of the law so clear to each man as that written in his heart? What sacrifices equal the self-denials which loving men and women make for one another? And what altar can be compared with the heart of a good man, on which God Himself accepts the sacrifice?

'The higher a man's conception of God, the better will he know Him. And the better he knows God, the nearer will he draw to Him, imitating His goodness, His mercy, and His love of man.

'Therefore, let him who sees the sun's whole light filling the world, refrain from blaming or despising the superstitious man, who in his own idol sees one ray of that same light. Let him not despise even the unbeliever who is blind and cannot see the sun at all.'

So spoke the Chinaman, the student of Confucius; and all who were present in the coffee-house were silent, and disputed no more as to whose faith was the best.

1893.

SOURCE:
https://www.marxists.org/archive/tolstoy/1893/the-coffeehouse-of-surat.html

---

A WORD FOR AUTUMN By A. A. Milne

This is the sort of urbane pleasantry in which British essayists are prolific and graceful. Alan Alexander Milne was born in 1882, went to Trinity College, Cambridge; was editor of The Granta (the leading undergraduate publication at Cambridge at that time); and plunged into the great whirlpool of London journalism. He was on the staff of Punch, 1906-14. He has now collected several volumes of charming essays, and has had considerable success as a playwright: his comedy, Mr. Pim Passes By, recently played a prosperous run in New York. "A Word for Autumn" is from his volume Not That It Matters.

LAST night the waiter put the celery on with the cheese, and I knew that summer was indeed dead. Other signs of autumn there may be—the reddening leaf, the chill in the early-morning air, the misty evenings—but none of these comes home to me so truly. There may be cool mornings in July; in a year of drought the leaves may change before their time; it is only with the first celery that summer is over.

I knew all along that it would not last. Even in April I was saying that winter would soon be here. Yet somehow it had begun to seem possible lately that a miracle might happen, that summer might drift on and on through the months—a final upheaval to crown a wonderful year. The celery settled that. Last night with the celery autumn came into its own.

There is a crispness about celery that is of the essence of October. It is as fresh and clean as a rainy day after a spell of heat. It crackles pleasantly in the mouth. Moreover it is excellent, I am told, for the complexion. One is always hearing of things which are good for the complexion, but there is no doubt that celery stands high on the list. After the burns and freckles of summer one is in need of something. How good that celery should be there at one's elbow.

A week ago—("A little more cheese, waiter")—a week ago I grieved for the dying summer. I wondered how I could possibly bear the waiting—the eight long months till May. In vain to comfort myself with the thought that I could get through more work in the winter undistracted by thoughts of cricket grounds and country houses. In vain, equally, to tell myself that I could stay in bed later in the mornings. Even the thought of after-breakfast pipes in front of the fire left me cold. But now, suddenly, I am reconciled to autumn. I see quite clearly that all good things must come to an end. The summer has been splendid, but it has lasted long enough. This morning I welcomed the chill in the air; this morning I viewed the falling leaves with cheerfulness; and this morning I said to myself, "Why, of course, I'll have celery for lunch." ("More bread, waiter.")

"Season of mists and mellow fruitfulness," said Keats, not actually picking out celery in so many words, but plainly including it in the general blessings of the autumn. Yet what an opportunity he missed by not concentrating on that precious root. Apples, grapes, nuts, and vegetable marrows he mentions specially—and how poor a selection! For apples and grapes are not typical of any month, so ubiquitous are they, vegetable marrows are vegetables pour rire and have no place in any serious consideration of the seasons, while as for nuts, have we not a national song which asserts distinctly, "Here we go gathering nuts in May"? Season of mists and mellow celery, then let it be. A pat of butter underneath the bough, a wedge of cheese, a loaf of bread and—Thou.

How delicate are the tender shoots unfolded layer by layer. Of what a whiteness is the last baby one of all, of what a sweetness his flavor. It is well that this should be the last rite of the meal—finis coronat opus—so that we may go straight on to the business of the pipe. Celery demands a pipe rather than a cigar, and it can be eaten better in an inn or a London tavern than in the home. Yes, and it should be eaten alone, for it is the only food which one really wants to hear oneself eat. Besides, in company one may have to consider the wants of others. Celery is not a thing to share with any man. Alone in your country inn you may call for the celery; but if you are wise you will see that no other traveler wanders into the room. Take warning from one who has learnt a lesson. One day I lunched alone at an inn, finishing with cheese and celery. Another traveler came in and lunched too. We did not speak—I was busy with my celery. From the other end of the table he reached across for the cheese. That was all right! it was the public cheese. But he also reached across for the celery—my private celery for which I owed. Foolishly—

you know how one does—I had left the sweetest and crispest shoots till the last, tantalizing myself pleasantly with the thought of them. Horror! to see them snatched from me by a stranger. He realized later what he had done and apologized, but of what good is an apology in such circumstances? Yet at least the tragedy was not without its value. Now one remembers to lock the door.

Yes, I can face the winter with calm. I suppose I had forgotten what it was really like. I had been thinking of the winter as a horrid wet, dreary time fit only for professional football. Now I can see other things—crisp and sparkling days, long pleasant evenings, cheery fires. Good work shall be done this winter. Life shall be lived well. The end of the summer is not the end of the world. Here's to October—and, waiter, some more celery.

SOURCE:
https://www.gutenberg.org/files/38280/38280-h/38280-h.htm#A_WORD_FOR_AUTUMN

VR NOTES 9

Virtual Philosophy

Professor Lane's Course Using VR Technology

ASSIGNMENT MODULE TEN | OCCAM'S RAZOR

CUBISM APPLICATION

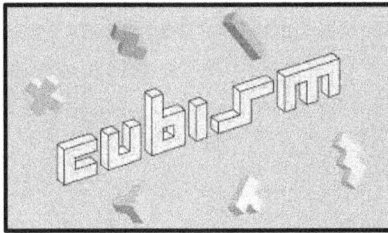

INSTRUCTIONS: See how many puzzles you can solve in Cubism VR. Keep trying even if you get frustrated. After achieving some success, read the following essays and think about how logic, spatial reasoning, and algorithmic thinking are important in successfully completing a specific project. Write a short essay providing three examples of how Occam's Razor works in principle. Feel free to be autobiographical in showing how a simpler (yet accurate and comprehensive) explanation is preferable over a more complex one. Be sure to post on your website and share with your classmates.

OCCAM'S RAZOR

one should not increase, beyond what is necessary, the number of entities required to explain anything

Occam's razor is a logical principle attributed to the mediaeval philosopher William of Occam (or Ockham). The principle states that one should not make more assumptions than the minimum needed. This principle is often called the principle of parsimony. It underlies all scientific modelling and theory building. It admonishes us to choose from a set of otherwise equivalent models of a given phenomenon the simplest one. In any given model, Occam's razor helps us to "shave off" those concepts, variables or constructs that are not really needed to explain the phenomenon. By doing that, developing the model will become much easier, and there is less chance of introducing inconsistencies, ambiguities and redundancies.

Though the principle may seem rather trivial, it is essential for model building because of what is known as the "underdetermination of theories by data". For a given set of observations or data, there is always an infinite number of possible models explaining those same data. This is because a model normally represents an infinite number of possible cases, of which the observed cases are only a finite subset. The non-observed cases are inferred by postulating general rules covering both actual and potential observations.

For example, through two data points in a diagram you can always draw a straight line, and induce that all further observations will lie on that line. However, you could also draw an infinite variety of the most complicated curves passing through those same two points, and these curves would fit the empirical data just as well. Only Occam's razor would in this case guide you in choosing the "straight" (i.e. linear) relation as best candidate model. A similar reasoning can be made for n data points lying in any kind of distribution.

Occam's razor is especially important for universal models such as the ones developed in General Systems Theory, mathematics or philosophy, because there the subject domain is of an unlimited complexity. If one starts with too complicated foundations for a theory that potentially encompasses the universe, the chances of getting any manageable model are very slim indeed. Moreover, the principle is sometimes the only remaining guideline when entering domains of such a high level of abstraction that no concrete tests or observations can decide between rival models. In mathematical modelling of systems, the principle can be made more concrete in the form of the principle of uncertainty maximization: from your data, induce that model which minimizes the number of additional assumptions.

This principle is part of epistemology, and can be motivated by the requirement of maximal simplicity of cognitive models. However, its significance might be extended to metaphysics if it is interpreted as saying that simpler models are more likely to be correct than complex ones, in other words, that "nature" prefers simplicity.

SOURCE: http://pespmc1.vub.ac.be/OCCAMRAZ.html

ELIMINATIVE MATERIALISM (ALSO CALLED ELIMINATIVISM)

is a materialist position in the philosophy of mind. Its primary claim is that people's common-sense understanding of the mind (or folk psychology) is false and that certain classes of mental states that most people believe in do not exist. Some eliminativists claim that no neural correlates will be found for many everyday psychological concepts, such as belief and desire, and that behaviour and experience can only be adequately explained on the biological level. Other versions entail the non-existence of conscious mental states such as pains and visual perceptions.

Eliminativism about a class of entities is the view that that class of entities does not exist. For example, atheism is eliminativist about God and other supernaturnatural entities; all forms of materialism are eliminativist about the soul; modern chemists are eliminativist about phlogiston; and modern physicists are eliminativist about the existence of ether. Eliminative materialism is the relatively new (1960s-70s) idea that certain classes of mental entities that commonsense takes for granted, such as beliefs, desires and the subjective sensation of pain, do not exist. The most common versions are eliminativism about propositional attitudes, as expressed by Paul and Pat Churchland, and eliminativism about qualia (subjective experience), as expressed by Daniel Dennett and Georges Rey.

Various arguments have been put forth both for and against eliminative materialism over the last forty years. Most of the arguments in favour of the view are based on the assumption that people's commonsense view of the mind is actually an implicit theory, to be compared and constrasted with other scientific theories as to its explanatory success, accuracy and ability to allow us to make correct predictions about the future. Eliminativists argue that, based on these and other criteria, commonsense "folk" psychology has failed and will eventually need to be replaced with explanations derived from the neurosciences. These philosophers therefore tend to emphasize the importance of neuroscientific research as well as developments in artificial intelligence to sustain their thesis.

Philosophers who argue against eliminativism may take several approaches. Some argue that folk psychology is not a theory and should not be compared to one. Others argue that folk psychology is, in fact, a theory and a very successful, even indispensable, one. Another view is that since eliminativism assumes the existence of the beliefs and other entities it seeks to "eliminate", it must be self-refuting.

Overview

Schematic overview: Some sciences can be reduced (blue). Theories that are in principle irreducible are eventually eliminated (orange).

Eliminativism maintains that the common-sense understanding of the mind is mistaken, and that the neurosciences will one day reveal that the mental states that are talked about in every day discourse, using words such as intend, believe, desire, and love, do not refer to anything real. Because of the inadequacy of natural languages, people mistakenly think that they have such beliefs and desires. Some eliminativists, such as the early Frank Jackson, claim that consciousness does not exist except as an epiphenomenon of brain function; others, such as Georges Rey, claim that the concept will eventually be eliminated as neuroscience progresses. Consciousness and folk psychology are separate issues and it is possible to take an eliminative stance on one but not the other. The roots of eliminativism go back to the writings of Wilfred Sellars, W.V. Quine, Paul Feyerabend, and Richard Rorty. The term "eliminative materialism" was first introduced by James Cornman in 1968 while describing a version of physicalism endorsed by Rorty. The later Ludwig Wittgenstein was also an important inspiration for eliminativism, particularly with his attack on "private objects" as "grammatical fictions".

Early eliminativists such as Rorty and Feyerabend often confused two different notions of the sort of elimination that the term eliminative materialism entailed. On the one hand, they claimed, the cognitive sciences that will ultimately give us a correct account of the workings of the mind will not employ terms that refer to common-sense mental states like beliefs and desires; these states will not be part of the ontology of a mature cognitive science. But critics immediately countered that this view was indistinguishable from the identity theory of mind. Quine himself wondered what exactly was so eliminative about eliminative materialism after all.

Is physicalism a repudiation of mental objects after all, or a theory of them? Does it repudiate the mental state of pain or anger in favour of its physical concomitant, or does it identify the mental state with a state of the physical organism (and so a state of the physical organism with the mental state)

On the other hand, the same philosophers also claimed that common-sense mental states simply do not exist. But critics pointed out that eliminativists could not have it both ways: either mental states exist and will ultimately be explained in terms of lower-level neurophysiological processes or they do not. Modern eliminativists have much more clearly expressed the view that mental phenomena simply do not exist and will eventually be eliminated from our thinking about the brain in the same way that demons have been eliminated from our thinking about mental illness and psychopathology.

During the late 1960s and early 1970s, eliminativism gained a wide variety of adherents because of the influence of scientific behaviourism. Proponents of this view, such as B.F. Skinner, often made parallels to previous pseudoscientific theories (such as that of the the the four humours, the phlogiston theory of combustion, and the vital force theory of life) that have all been successfully eliminated in attempting to establish their thesis about the nature of the mental. In these cases, science has not produced more detailed versions or reductions of these theories, but rejected them altogether as obsolete. Behaviorists argued that folk psychology is already obsolete and should be replaced by descriptions of stimulus and response patterns. Such views were eventually abandoned. According to Quine and the Churchlands, it will take decades before folk psychology is finally replaced by real science.

Eliminativism is not only motivated by philosophical considerations, but is also a prediction about what form future scientific theories will take. Eliminativist philosophers therefore tend to be very concerned with the data coming from the relevant brain and cognitive sciences. In addition, because eliminativism is essentially predictive in nature, different theorists can, and often do, make different predictions about which aspects of folk psychology will be eliminated from our folk psychological vocabulary. None of these philosophers are eliminativists "tout court".

Today, the eliminativist view is most closely associated with the philosophers Paul and Patricia Churchland, who deny the existence of propositional attitudes (a subclass of intentional states), and with Daniel Dennett, who is generally considered to be an eliminativist about qualia and phenomenal aspects of consciousness. One way to summarize the difference between the Churchlands's views and Dennett's view is that the Churchlands are eliminativists when it comes to propositional attitudes, but reductionists concerning qualia, while Dennett is a reductionist with respect to propositional attitudes, and an eliminativist concerning qualia.

Arguments for eliminativism

Problems with folk theories

Eliminativists such as Paul and Patricia Churchland argue that folk psychology is a fully developed but non-formalized theory of human behavior. It is used to explain and make predictions about human mental states and behaviour. This view is often referred to as the theory-theory, for it is a theory which theorizes the existence of an unacknowledged theory. As a theory in the scientific sense, eliminativists maintain, folk psychology needs to be evaluated on the basis of its predictive power and explanatory success as a research program for the investigation of the mind/brain.

Such eliminativists have developed different arguments to show that folk psychology is a seriously mistaken theory and needs to be abolished. They argue that folk psychology excludes from its purview or has traditionally been mistaken about many important mental phenomena that can, and are, being examined and explained by modern neurosciences. Some examples are dreaming, consciousness, mental disorders, learning processes and memory abilities. Furthermore, they argue, folk psychology's development in the last 2,500 years has not been very significant and it is therefore a stagnating theory. The ancient Greeks already had a folk psychology comparable to ours. But in contrast to this lack of development, the neurosciences are a rapidly progressing science complex that, in their view, can explain many cognitive processes that folk psychology cannot.

Folk psychology retains characteristics of now obsolete theories or legends from the past. Ancient societies tried to explain the physical mysteries of nature by ascribing mental conditions to them in such statements as "the sea is angry". Gradually, these everyday folk psychological explanations were replaced by more efficient scientific descriptions. Today, eliminativists argue, there is no reason not to accept an effective scientific account of our cognitive abilities. If we had such an explanation, then there would be no need for folk-psychological explanations of behaviour, and the latter would be eliminated the same way as the mythological explanations the ancients used.

Another line of argument is the meta-induction based on what eliminativists view as the disastrous historical record of folk theories in general. Our ancient pre-scientific "theories" of folk biology, folk physics and folk cosmology have all proven to be radically wrong. Why shouldn't the same thing happen in the case of folk psychology? There seems no logical basis, to the eliminativist, for making an exception just because folk psychology has lasted longer and is more intuitive or instinctively plausible than the other folk theories. Indeed, the eliminativists warn, considerations of intuitive plausibility may be precisely the result of the deeply entrenched nature in society of folk psychology itself. It may be that our beliefs and other such states are as theory-laden as external perceptions and hence our intuitions will tend to be biased in favour of them.

Specific problems with folk psychology

Much of folk psychology involves the attribution of intentional states (also known as propositional attitudes). Eliminativists point out that these states are generally ascribed syntactic and semantic properties. An example of this is the language of thought hypothesis, which attributes a discrete, combinatorial syntax and other linguistic properties to these mental phenomena. Eliminativists argue that such discrete and combinatorial characteristics have no place in the neurosciences, which speak of action potentials, spiking frequencies, and other effects which are continuous and distributed in nature. Hence, the syntactic structures which are assumed by folk psychology can have no place in such a structure as the brain. Against this there have been two responses: on the one hand, there are philosophers who deny that mental states are linguistic in nature and see this as a straw man argument; on the other, those who subscribe to something like a language of thought assert that the mental states can be multiply realized and that functional characterizations are just higher-level characterizations of what's happening at the physical level.

It has also been urged against folk psychology that the intentionality of mental states like belief imply that they have semantic qualities. Specifically, their meaning is determined by the things that they are about in the external world. This makes it difficult to explain how they can play the causal roles that they are supposed to in cognitive processes.

In recent years, this latter argument has been fortified by the theory of connectionism. Many connectionist models of the brain have been developed in which the processes of language learning and other forms of representation are highly distributed and parallel. This would tend to indicate that there is no need for such discrete and semantically-endowed entities as beliefs and desires.

SOURCE:
https://www.cs.mcgill.ca/~rwest/wikispeedia/wpcd/wp/e/Eliminative_materialism.htm

VR NOTES 10

Virtual Philosophy

Professor Lane's Course Using VR Technology

ASSIGNMENT MODULE ELEVEN | COMPASSIONATE ETHICS

HENRY VR FILM

INSTRUCTIONS: First, watch the movie Henry, one of the very first VR films released on Oculus and then read the following two essays. After this write an essay answering the following question: "How large is your circle of compassion?" In other words, define your ethical system in terms of geometry: does it include just family? Just friends? Or does it go beyond the obvious? Other nations? Animals? Etc. This isn't a right and wrong query, but rather an autobiographical exploration of where you place your ethical system and why. Be sure to explain the rationale behind your own moral system. The essay should be at least 500 words or more. Use examples whenever possible. Post on your website and then share, if comfortable, with your classmates.

THE SCIENCE OF VALUES: THE MORAL LANDSCAPE
by Sam Harris

Reviewed by James W. Diller and Andrew E. Nuzzolilli

In *The Moral Landscape,* Sam Harris (2010) proposes that science can be used to identify values, which he defines as "facts that can be scientifically understood: regarding positive and negative social emotions, retributive impulses, the effects of specific laws and social institutions on human relationships, the neurophysiology of happiness and suffering, etc." (pp. 1–2). Harris argues that scientific principles are appropriately applied in this domain because "human well-being entirely depends on events in the world and on states of the human brain. Consequently, there must be scientific truths known about it" (p. 3). Although readers of this journal would have few problems with the assertion that behavior (here, reports of well-being and correlated responses) changes as a function of environmental events, the role of the neurophysiological correlates of these responses has been a point of debate within the conceptual literature of behavior analysis (e.g., Elcoro, 2008; Reese, 1996; Schaal, 2003).

The Moral Landscape represents an important contribution to a scientific discussion of morality. It explicates the determinants of moral behavior for a popular audience, placing causality in the external environment and in the organism's correlated neurological states. The contemporary science of behavior analysis has and will continue to contribute to this discussion, originating with Skinner's seminal works Beyond Freedom and Dignity (1971) and Walden Two (1976). Neither book is explicitly a treatise on morality, but both are attempts to introduce behavioral science to a broader audience. The behavior-analytic approach (which is largely compatible with Harris's efforts in *The Moral Landscape*) supports the superiority of a scientific approach to life, including questions of morality. Skinner (1976), for example, highlighted the importance of the experimenting culture to identify practices that were effective (cf. Baum, 2005). Tacit within behavior analysis is the expectation that a scientific worldview can and will improve the quality of life. Consistent with this view, Harris suggests that the currently accepted determinants of morality (e.g., religion, faith) are not what society ought to espouse. Instead, he proposes that scientific inquiry into morality as its own subject would enhance global levels of well-being. From a behavioral perspective, the study of morality is necessarily the study of behavior, including the contexts in which it occurs and the environmental events of which it is a function. Analysis in this framework may allow the successful identification of the variables that control moral behavior, and, ultimately, the development of cultural practices to increase its occurrence.

The Moral Landscape is a recent contribution to a collection of books (e.g., Dawkins, 2006; Harris, 2005; Hitchens, 2007; Sagan, 2006) that subject the claims of religion to the same standard of empirical rigor that other epistemologies (e.g., science) must abide by. Dawkins (2006), for example, criticizes the appeal to supernatural gods as explanatory agents and takes issue with the privileged place of religion within societal discourse. Harris echoes and expands on these concerns in The Moral Landscape.

Collectively, these authors take issue with the notion of nonoverlapping magisteria (NOMA; Gould, 1999), which is the assertion that science and religion are both valid systems of knowledge, and that neither discipline can inform the other. Behavior analysts take issue with the notion that scientific behavior and religious behavior are egalitarian (see Galuska, 2003, for suggestions about successful navigation of NOMA by behavior analysts). Skinner (1987) commented, "Science, not religion, has taught me my most useful values, among them intellectual honesty. It is better to go without answers than to accept those that merely resolve puzzlement" (p. 12). Although religion may be effective at inducing behavioral change among its followers, it continues to have unintended effects that, to borrow Harris's analogy, reach the depths of the moral landscape. Hitchens (2007) makes a subtitular claim that "religion poisons everything," supporting his thesis with discussions of demonstrably negative outcomes associated with religious practice, discussing examples of how religion leads to poorer states of human health and impedes social progress. As an alternative, he proposes a rational, scientific view of the world, which Harris applies to the study of morality.

Because they are members of a relatively small discipline, it may be beneficial for behavior analysts to align themselves with and support the authors of these works, garnering attention from the controversial coverage from popular media outlets that writers such as Dawkins and Harris regularly elicit. Perhaps controversial exposure is better than no exposure at all, especially when behavior analysis can enable the development of the hypothetical secular society that Harris, Dawkins, Hitchens, and Sagan call for. Indeed, behavior analysis may be the only discipline that can identify and establish reinforcers to motivate prosocial, so-called moral, human behavior in the absence of organized religion.

It is noteworthy that no psychologist has tackled the problem of secular values alongside these authors in spite of the contradictory facts that religion presents about human nature, facts that take away from the value of our discipline. Indeed, much of the rich "prescientific" vocabulary that inhibits psychology from becoming a natural science is either religious or metaphysical in nature (Schlinger, 2004). It is imperative for the validation of the field of psychology, as well as behavior analysis by association, to be a part of this modern empiricist movement championed by Harris.

Harris's argument unfolds in an introduction and five subsequent chapters. In the introduction, he defines his title concept of the moral landscape as a hypothetical space representing human well-being, encompassing all human experiences. This space contains the well-being of members of all cultures and groups of individuals on the planet. The peaks of this landscape are the heights of prosperity, and the valleys represent the depths of human suffering. The goal of plotting the cartography of this landscape is to maximize "the well-being of conscious creatures" (i.e., humans) which "must translate at some point into facts about brains and their interactions with the world at large" (p. 11). For Harris, the brain is the locus of interest. We believe that it is possible to recast the argument into one about whole organisms—with correlated neurological states, perhaps—interacting with their environment to determine behavior. This scientific approach to human behavior, with a goal of improving the welfare of living organisms, is consistent with the application of behavior analysis to bring about societal change (e.g., Baer, Wolf, & Risley, 1968; Skinner, 1971, 1978).

In the subsequent chapters of his book, Harris makes the case for applying scientific thinking to determine human values. Chapter 1 outlines the knowable nature of moral truths, suggesting that they are subject to scientific (rather than religious) inquiry. In Chapter 2, Harris tackles the topics of good and evil, suggesting that these terms may be outmoded; instead, the goal of both religion and science should be to determine ways to maximize human well-being. In the third chapter, Harris explores the neurological correlates of belief, tracing the complex sets of behavior back to brain activity. In the fourth chapter, he examines the role of religious faith in contemporary society, suggesting that a scientific approach may lead to an increase in overall well-being. The final chapter outlines a plan for future work, disentangling science and philosophy, and offering an optimistic picture about the use of science to improve the human condition. In sum, Harris presents a cogent argument for the application of scientific principles to identify moral principles and values. In what follows, we describe his arguments and some intersections with the behavioral approach to this topic.

Defining Morality

The crux of Harris's argument is that the well-being of conscious creatures should be the paramount consideration when determining whether an action is morally correct or incorrect. Harris uses the term conscious creature extensively in formulating his science of morality. Although he does not provide an explicit definition of consciousness, his use seems to be at odds with the behavioral approach to this construct. For Harris, consciousness seems to be a property of the brain, discoverable by explorations in neuroscience. In contrast, Skinner (1945) suggested that, when defining psychological terms, it is useful to identify the conditions under which those terms are used, and the history of the verbal community that produces that usage. Consistent with this analysis, Schlinger (2008) proposed that consciousness is best understood with a focus on the behaviors that are associated with the use of the word consciousness (e.g., self-talk, private behavior), rather than the study of the reified thing itself.

Consciousness, defined as a set of verbal behavior, is a prerequisite for a discussion of morality. Verbal behavior is required for us to evaluate our own subjective well-being in relation to the well-being of others, allowing us to identify the relative "goodness" or "badness" of each; such an analysis is necessarily dependent on verbal behavior. Indeed, in other media (cf. The Richard Dawkins Foundation, 2011), Harris has suggested that a universe of rocks could not define a science of morality, because consciousness (i.e., a verbal repertoire about one's own behavior) is required to discuss subjective experience.

When providing a definition for the well-being that should be promoted, Harris likens this concept to physical health, noting,

Indeed the difference between a healthy person and a dead one is about as clear and consequential a distinction as we ever make in science. The difference between the heights of human fulfillment and the depths of human misery are no less clear even if new frontiers await us in both directions. (p. 12)

With this definition, it is possible to cast a wide net and capture a multitude of human behaviors and conditions. Harris suggests that, much like physical health, well-being eludes concise definition. Although the use of well-being is not precisely operationalized, he does define morality as "the principles of behavior that allow people to flourish" (p. 19). This phrasing is likely the closest to an operational definition of morality that is possible without undertaking the scientific analysis that Harris proposes in which fundamental principles to increase moral behavior could be discovered. The use of flourishing human life as a criterion for morality may be consistent with Skinner's (1945) approach to evaluating terms as a function of the conditions in which they occur: Morality, for Harris, may be evident only when well-being is enhanced. The next step of the analysis would be to systematically identify the conditions that give rise to that flourishing human life, exploring the antecedents (e.g., having basic needs met, education, leisure time) and the consequences thereof. Behavioral technologies such as functional analysis (e.g., Iwata, Dorsey, Slifer, Bauman, & Richman, 1982/1994) may provide the tools required to successfully carry out this work.

A major premise of Harris's work is that there is variability in the degree of "goodness" that individuals experience in life, and this variability can be accounted for by brain states and events in the external environment. If one accepts the distinction between "the good life" and "the bad life" and the idea that there are lawful patterns and factors that contribute to each of these outcomes (i.e., a deterministic framework), it allows the development of a scientific view of morality. This scientific view, according to Harris, stands as an alternative to traditional religious perspectives. Harris writes, "There is simply no question that how we speak about human values—and how we study or fail to study the relevant phenomena at the level of the brain—will profoundly influence our collective future" (p. 25). This theme can be found in the writings of Skinner (1971), who suggested that the scientific approach to the world's practical problems can allow the development of solutions to those problems. Although Harris's argument is framed in the language of neuroscience instead of Skinner's behavioral perspective, a similarly pragmatic approach shows through.

The introduction of Harris's book is wholly devoted to the qualification of values as scientific facts: verifiable statements about organisms and the environment around them. This argument, that utterances reflect or are symbolic of environmental events, should be familiar to those who are familiar with Skinner's conceptualization of a verbal community. If we are to accept that utterances about "moral behavior," "morality," or "ethics" are not importantly different from other verbal behavior, then they too can become a topic for scientific inquiry. Such an analysis could evaluate the conditions under which this verbal behavior is emitted and the consequences thereof. With this understanding of the contingencies of reinforcement that promote and maintain these responses, it would be possible to shape the moral behavior of individuals or groups.

Harris posits that "science can, in principle, help us understand what we should do and should want—and, therefore, what other people should do and should want in order to live the best lives possible" (p. 28). This is congruent with Skinner's acceptance of the value judgment (i.e., is or ought statements) as a tool to reveal the oftentimes subtle contingencies that control social behavior. Harris describes well-being as the conceptual basis for morality and values, stating, "there must be a science of morality ... because the well-being of conscious creatures depends upon how the universe is, altogether" (p. 28). Bringing morality into the natural world makes it amenable to scientific study, and

Harris's book complements the work that behavior analysts have done with respect to questions of morality.

The behavior-analytic approach to values and morals has its origin with Skinner, who suggested that things that individuals call good are reinforcing, and that "any list of values is a list of reinforcers" (1953, p. 35). When describing Skinner's approach, Ruiz and Roche (2007) commented that "it is important to provide translations of value statements in functional terms in order to reveal the relevant contingencies of reinforcement" (p. 4). Thus, as with the discussion of consciousness above, the conditions under which particular behaviors are morally correct or incorrect must be considered. This functional approach may expand on Harris's proposed science of values and make it more acceptable to a behavioral audience.

Distinguishing Between Philosophical Positions on Morality

A large portion of Harris's book differentiates between the religious notions of values and morality and the scientific principles thereof. Harris suggests that religious concerns about morality are related to human well-being. In Chapter 1, he describes an agenda of finding scientific truth about questions of morality. To deal with the relative unpopularity of his approach (Harris reports that more people in contemporary American society believe that morality should stem from religious than scientific inquiries), he asserts that consensus and truth are not the same thing: "One person can be right, and everyone else can be wrong. Consensus is a guide to discovering what is going on in the world, but that is all that it is. Its presence or absence in no way constrains what may or may not be true" (p. 31). Harris reports that 57% of Americans believe that preventing homosexual marriage is a moral imperative (p. 53), a clear example of a common belief that impairs the progression of well-being.

With respect to differences between perspectives of different groups, Harris writes, "those who do not share our scientific goals have no influence on scientific discourse whatsoever; but, for some reason, people who do not share our moral goals render us incapable of even speaking about moral truth" (p. 34). Here, Harris is suggesting that religious beliefs, which may be incorrect according to other epistemological systems (e.g., science), prevent other systems from declaring them to be incorrect. However, religious belief systems do comment on the "truth" of empirical inquiries, a double standard with which Harris takes issue, and a concern that is expressed by other authors such as Dawkins (2006). The ability of science to comment on affairs related to religion and morality has the potential for the further advancement of human well-being via the development of new ideas and technologies. Without a scientific response to these issues, progress seems less likely.

To determine the merits of given philosophical systems, one can adopt a relativistic position. Relativism is the belief that points of view have no absolute truth. This tradition is largely a by-product of scientific skepticism, and can be just as harmful to a science of morality as any religious doctrine. By Harris's account, moral relativism is endemic throughout the scientific community. This is problematic for the development of the theoretical moral landscape because historically science has "had no opinion" on moral issues, which Harris ascribes to a fear of retribution by religious groups, political agendas, or intellectual laziness; he objects to the continuance of this harmful tradition. Harris suggests that relativism is accepted as an absolute position and is not subject to a contextual analysis (that relativism itself should require). He points out that this absolute acceptance of a relativistic worldview is fundamentally contradictory to the principle of relativism itself. If we are to believe that the practices in question (examples that Harris highlights include female genital mutilation and subjugation of women) are correct in the relevant cultural and historical time period, this belief must also be cast as relative and changeable, which it generally is not. In addition, Harris suggests that relativistic positions may lead to misguided beliefs about how to improve human well-being.

Perhaps at odds with Harris's analysis, Skinner suggested that there are multiple sets of values that may emerge across cultural settings: "Each culture has its own set of goods, and what is good in one culture may not be good in another" (1971, p. 122). The reinforcers (i.e., values) identified across cultures necessarily vary as a function of the different physical and cultural environments in which the moral systems develop. For Skinner, the criterion by which to evaluate the goodness of a cultural practice is the degree to which it promotes survival of the society. Thus, although there are potentially many different ways for a culture to survive, there may be some that maximize the level of well-being of the individuals and the group. Skinner's position is pragmatic, but has garnered criticism from within the behavior-analytic community (e.g., Ruiz & Roche, 2007). Critiques of the cultural survivability criterion emphasize the impossibility of determining which cultural practices will, in fact, enhance survivability without definite knowledge of the future. Ruiz and Roche (2007) called "for behavior analysts to consider seriously where we as a community stand on relativism and to discuss openly and thoroughly the criteria we will use in adopting ethical principles" (p. 11). Harris's position of rejecting moral relativism in favor of universal principles to promote well-being may help to inform the behavior-analytic discourse.

Belief

After establishing that our beliefs can, indeed, be incorrect or somehow inconsistent with reality, Harris qualifies his argument. Citing research conducted in his own laboratory on the neuroscience of belief, he posits that there is no difference between what we deem to be "knowledge," "belief," and "truth," and these utterances can be attributed to functionally equivalent neurological correlates. Indeed, the brain's endogenous reward systems reinforce beliefs and utterances that we deem "true" with positive emotional valence. He writes,

When we believe a proposition to be true, it is as though we have taken it in hand as part of our extended self, we are saying in effect, "This is mine. I can use this. This fits my view of the world." (p. 121)

This evidence from neuroscience supports the notion that values, knowledge, belief, and truth belong to the same class of verbal behavior, but may not necessarily share discriminative stimuli (Skinner, 1945). Taking this research to its logical conclusion, one can suggest that an individual's learning history would dictate which beliefs, truths, or bits of knowledge could fit into a person's worldview. By Harris's account, we dislike information that contradicts our worldviews as much as we dislike being lied to. With this bias established, it is easier to see precisely how maladaptive or harmful beliefs can be propagated.

Organism–Environment interactions

In Chapter 2, Harris suggests that an understanding of the human brain and its states will allow an understanding of forces that improve society (e.g., prosocial behavior). He writes,

As we better understand the brain, we will increasingly understand all of the forces ... that allow friends and strangers to collaborate successfully on the common projects of civilization. Understanding ourselves in this way and using the knowledge to improve human life, will be among the most important challenges to science in the decades to come. (pp. 55–56)

Cooperation is one of the mechanisms through which values may come about, and Harris contends that "there may be nothing more important than human cooperation" (p. 55). Conceptualizing the failures of cooperation as the everyday grievances of theft, deception, and violence, it is plain to see how failing to cooperate can be an impediment to human well-being and moral development.

Harris emphasizes the role of consequences in the formation of values, suggesting that

all questions of value depend upon the possibility of experiencing such value. Without potential consequences at the level of experience—happiness, suffering, joy, despair etc.—all talk of value is empty ... even within religion, therefore, consequences and conscious states remain the foundation of all values. (p. 62)

In this quote, Harris suggests the power of consequences to effect change in behavior. In so doing, Harris takes morality out of his context of neurological events and places it into an environmental framework. Although he does acknowledge the behavior–environment interaction as a cause for moral responding, a behavior-analytic approach would go further, emphasizing the power of consequences to increase or decrease (i.e., reinforce or punish) the likelihood that moral behavior would occur. It is the consequences of behavior that make it more or less likely to occur in a selectionist framework (cf. Glenn & Madden, 1995), and those same consequences seem to work similarly at the neurological level (e.g., Stein, Xue, & Belluzzi, 1994). Thus, it is the interaction between the environment and the organism that leads to the development of any behavior, including moral responses and those associated with varying degrees of well-being.

Taking this environment-based approach, Harris presents contemporary research from neuroscience throughout his book. After describing the neurological precursors and correlates of behavior, he dismisses the notion of free will, citing additional biological data to suggest that it is the brain—and not an agent of free will—that is responsible for behavior. He makes a familiar argument for a deterministic framework, in which the historical and contemporary environments (including neurological states) are responsible for behavior. After dismantling free will, Harris describes ramifications for the justice system. With this knowledge, we can no longer hold people accountable for their actions because they are determined by historical and contemporary events. This view negates a justice system based on punishment or retribution. Consistent with a behavioral position (e.g., Chiesa, 2003), Harris suggests that, with increased knowledge about the brain (for which we may be able to substitute behavior without losing any meaning, because the brain necessarily belongs to a complete organism), reforms of the justice system may be necessary. A reformed justice system would be more compassionate based on its more accurate understanding of causes of behavior (i.e., the environment and biological states). Harris takes this position to an extreme, proposing that it may even be immoral to fail to consider environmental and biological factors within the context of the justice system. Here, there is a fundamental compatibility between the approach that Harris is advocating and a behavioral worldview.

Indeed, the understanding of proximate and ultimate causes that precede any event are essential to making logically coherent arguments, not just from the perspective of the justice system but in understanding the behavior of all organisms. The ultimate cause of many reprehensible human behaviors lies in the distant evolutionary past. Proximate causes can be shaped over the course of single lifetimes and may covary with environmental stimuli (Mayr, 1961; Skinner, 1981). For the purposes of Harris's argument, we will agree that the nervous system and the brain are proximate causes of behavior, but these were influenced by both the evolutionary history of the species and the learning environment of the individual (cf. Schlinger & Poling, 1998, pp. 39–41). A more thorough discussion of ultimate cause may be a better locus to develop the science of moral behavior which he calls for.

A Program For Changing Moral Behavior

If Harris's claims that morality is knowable through scientific processes are true (and, based on his arguments in the book, we, at least, are convinced), behavior analysis ought to be at the forefront of the emerging science of morality. As a discipline, behavior analysis is uniquely positioned to deal with matters that span the continuum of well-being and suffering (i.e., the peaks and valleys of Harris's moral landscape). Behavior analysis has a history of developing and using demonstrably effective behavior-change procedures. Because Harris's neurological correlates of well-being are isomorphic with human behavior, the methods of experimental and applied behavior analysis could be used to support the type of work that Harris proposes.

In the first chapter of the book, Harris outlines three primary directions that work in the science of morality can take: (a) Explain why people engage in particular behavior "in the name of morality"; (b) "determine which patterns of thought and behavior we should follow in the name of 'morality'"; and (c) convince people "who are committed to silly and harmful patterns of thought and behavior in the name of 'morality' to break these commitments and to live better lives" (p. 49). Behavior analysts have the conceptual framework and behavior-change techniques to potentially make meaningful contributions to each of these goals.

Conclusions

In *The Moral Landscape*, Harris begins to develop a science of morality that he believes could be used to maximize the well-being of humans. Although his approach to morality is largely grounded in neuroscience (rather than the study of the whole organism), he does present an environment-based approach to morality to a wide readership, continuing in the tradition of other recent works that have espoused secular worldviews (e.g., Dawkins, 2006; Hitchens, 2007). Harris's approach to the development of the science of morality is largely consistent with the behavioral approach; for him, as for behavior analysts, morality is behavior, and that behavior is subject to environmental (and biological) manipulation.

As part of his work, Harris describes the need to produce change in methods for producing change in moral behavior; the discipline of behavior analysis is ideally suited to contribute to this mission. The application of behavioral techniques to socially significant problems has been a hallmark of behavior analysis ever since Baer et al. (1968) laid the foundations of applied behavior analysis. Behavior change has been demonstrated from the level of the individual to the level of society, and these same principles could be applied to moral behavior, as described by Harris, to promote universal well-being. No other discipline matches behavior analysis in its scientific understanding of behavior or its tools to modify it. If Harris is correct that science should take an active role in determining human values, behavior analysts must be a part of that conversation.

SOURCE:
https://www.ncbi.nlm.nih.gov/pmc/articles/PMC3501430/

Behav Anal. 2012 Fall; 35(2): 265–273.

CONSCIENCE: THE ORIGINS OF MORAL INTUITION
Patricia Churchland

Reviewed by: Karen R. Koenig

"Churchland's take on conscience is likely messier than most of us will find comfort in, yearning as we do for moral clarity and certainty in order to make our decisions easier and put our conscience at rest."

Patricia S. Churchland, founder of neurophilosophy, is that rare author who can write a book about a deep and profound subject such as conscience and still manage to make it down to earth, accessible, and even humorous at times.

For readers not familiar with neurophilosophy, it means exactly what it sounds like: informing philosophic thinking through the exploration and application of scientific study, especially in neurobiology and evolutionary psychology. While paying homage to the development of morality through reason, cultural norms, and religion, Churchland's money is on what she calls the "whole-brain" function: "biology—instincts, learning, problem solving, and constraint satisfaction."

Churchland asks and answers questions central to understanding conscience and its origins: What is the purpose of feelings in human attachment? What part do caring, personality, and reputation play in the development of personal ethics? What facets of the brain are involved in forming judgments about right and wrong?

The book begins with a historical journey to understand how previous ages grappled with the slippery subject of morality. The Greeks, best illustrated by Plato and Aristotle, lacked a single word for "conscience." It was deemed con scientia by the Romans, meaning "knowledge of the community standards," though both ethnic groups recognized that conscience does not always mean adhering to these standards and sometimes even involves battling against them. The author also explores conscience through the lens of Christianity, Buddhism and Confucianism, theologians such as Martin Luther and philosophers such as Immanuel Kant.

Churchland's working formulation of conscience is: "an individual's judgment about what is morally right or wrong, typically, but not always, reflecting some standard of a group to which the individual feels attached." Factored into her description of conscience are the "feelings that urge us in a general direction, and judgment that shapes the urge into a specific action."

The author explains why we are wired and socially driven to care about others and why human infants are born so helpless compared to those of other species. She maintains that "mammalian ancestors were adapted for sociality" and that "in the evolution of the mammalian brain, feelings of pleasure and pain supporting self-survival were supplemented and repurposed to motivate affiliative behavior." Simply put, "the range of myself was extended to include my babies."

Add to this expanded circuitry the hormone oxytocin, which promotes social attachment and caring, especially for mates and infants, and the stage was set for empathy to occur as "an ever-present factor in how humans decide what accords with the demands of conscience." Churchland goes on to make the case that "neural wiring for attachment and bonding provides the motivational and emotional platform for sociality, which enables a scaffolding of social practices, moral inhibitions, and norms."

The fact that humans possess far larger and more complex cortical circuitry than other mammals enabled them to engage in what Churchland calls Big Learning. Larger brains required more food so that humans learned to cook to feed themselves, priming the evolutionary pump. Larger brains developed more distinct functions and led humans to become more flexible and, therefore, more adaptive to different situations. Flexibility, in turn, made them better able to survive and flourish.

This process is facilitated by the reward system's neurotransmitters dopamine and serotonin, which perform a crucial role in reinforcing what we desire and fear, moving us toward what brings pleasure and away from what causes pain. Additionally, Churchland describes how personality factors and social attitudes strongly influence what we view as good or bad.

Some of the most fascinating sections of the book (especially in this polarized political climate) include twin studies on heritability and brain research on the marked differences between the brains of conservatives and liberals. Churchland also delves into a nuanced discussion of psychopaths diagnosed as lacking empathy and non-psychopaths who have Anti-Social Personality Disorder. At the other end of the spectrum, she describes what happens when "moral behavior knows no limits, when it is uncontrolled," which is called scrupulosity, a type of Obsessive-Compulsive Disorder.

Churchland believes that conscience works best when we are in balance, no easy task when we are prone to go to great lengths to hide truth from ourselves. Sifting through philosophies such as Utilitarianism and Kantianism and debates about the role that reason and free will play in morality, her take on conscience is likely messier than most of us will find comfort in, yearning as we do for moral clarity and certainty in order to make our decisions easier and put our conscience at rest. Churchland's final chapter brings the whole discussion home and covers what works and doesn't work to enhance morality in our own lives and to improve our criminal justice system. One approach to achieving balance is modeling ourselves after others whom we respect and admire. Other recommendations for individuals include practicing honesty and avoiding self-deceit, arrogance, and certitude plus developing positive habits, also known as virtues, such as kindness, courage, patience and compassion which become our foundation in making moral decisions and choices. Socially conscious, Churchland also tasks us with creating a world that favors "decency, respect and kindness." She seems to be saying that because we have the neurobiology to fashion such a benevolent environment, it is time to find the will to make it happen.

Karen R. Koenig, MEd, LCSW, is a psychotherapist, psychology of eating expert, and eight-book international, award-winning author. Her most recent book is Words to Eat By: Using the Power of Self-talk to Transform Your Relationship with Food and Your Body (Turner Publishing, 2021).

SOURCE:
https://www.nyjournalofbooks.com/book-review/conscience-origins-moral-intuition

VR NOTES 11

Virtual Philosophy

Professor Lane's Course Using VR Technology

ASSIGNMENT MODULE TWELVE | ARTIFICIAL INTELLIGENCE

VIRTUAL VIRTUAL REALITY VR

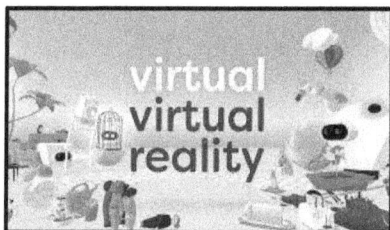

INSTRUCTIONS: Try to see if you can solve the Virtual Virtual Reality game and see where you end up. The VR app is designed to be strangely weird and disorienting, providing a glimpse into how A.I. is less about "artificial intelligence and more akin to an "alien intelligence" than anything else. Read the summary of Ray Kurzweil's famous book, The Singularity is Near. Here is the question I wish for you to ponder and answer to the best of your ability. What specific changes will A.I. make in your life in the next ten years that would change how you live your day-to-day life? Secondly, what changes in the future do wish to happen? Finally, what fears do you have about A.I.? Post your responses to these questions on your website. The sky is the limit.

THE SINGULARITY IS NEAR SUMMARY AND REVIEW

Ray Kurzweil

Has *The Singularity Is Near* by Ray Kurzweil been sitting on your reading list? Pick up the key ideas in the book with this quick summary.

Do you remember the scene in The Matrix, in which Neo has a program uploaded to his brain and, in an instant, he "knows" kung fu? What would life be like if you could upload knowledge just like a basic software program?

As these book summary will show, technology is evolving ever faster; in just a few decades, technological advances will enable us to transcend our biological shackles to overcome aging and disease.

In this new world, uploading a program to your brain will seem quaint. Technology will have become so advanced that it will mark a whole new era: a "singularity" in which computers will be billions of times smarter than all of humanity combined, and biology and technology will be one and the same.

This era isn't hundreds of years away, either. It's near.

In this summary of *The Singularity Is Near* by Ray Kurzweil, you'll learn

how DNA will be used to build supercomputers; why, in the future, you won't have to worry about sunburns; and how a few years from now, anyone can become a Spock.

The Singularity Is Near Key Idea #1:

Evolution is picking up speed. Each development builds and moves faster ahead than the last. Think about how many major technological changes your grandparents may have witnessed during their lifetimes. Now, think about the changes you've seen over just the last 15 years.

Stunning how far technology has advanced in such a short period of time, right?

It's evident that, as time passes, things are changing more rapidly. History tells us that the rate of change has been growing exponentially.

Roughly 3.8 billion years ago, single-celled life on earth evolved slowly. It took some 2 billion years for multicellular organisms to emerge.

Yet gradually, the process of evolution gained momentum. For example, there were only 200 million years between the first mammals and the evolution of Homo sapiens.

If you were to draw a graph showing major evolutionary development on earth, you'd see that evolution does indeed move faster with the passing of time. The same can be said for the rate of technological evolution.

Technological development is also accelerating. Some 50,000 years ago, discoveries such as making fire were few and far between, occuring every 1,000 years or so. Compare this rate with today, where it's a challenge to list the gadgets and revelations of just last year.

Importantly, the returns of this accelerating process of evolution are also accelerating.

For instance, computer speed in cost per unit doubled every three years between 1910 and 1950, then every two years between 1950 and 1966; today, it's doubling each year.

This exponential development in technology is known as the "Law of Accelerating Returns."

We know that the greatest triumphs in each stage of development help to form the next. For example, biological evolution resulted in Homo sapiens; humans then invented technology, and the best technologies are used to develop even better technologies.

It follows then that eventually, supersmart computers will be able to design superior technologies themselves and in doing so, further speed up technological evolution.

The Singularity Is Near Key Idea #2:

Computers are making leaps and bounds in speed and processing power. DNA computing is near. Computers are evolving rapidly, especially as ever-shrinking silicon components improve their performance. But even silicon has its limitations.

Very thin silicon components leak electricity, and densely wired chips overheat, which lowers efficiency. To counter these problems, new technologies are already in the pipeline.

One such invention is nanotube technology, an invention that will significantly speed computer calculations.

Nanotubes are tiny cylinders made out of sheets of carbon atoms. They are excellent candidates as chip components, because electrons pass through nanotubes far more easily than through silicon-based transistors.

The result is that data can be transmitted more quickly. In fact, computer scientist Peter Burke says the theoretical speed limit for a nanotube transistor computer would reach 100 times that of a conventional computer!

Another advantage is that many minuscule nanotubes can fit onto a single chip, speeding performance while avoiding the losses typical of scaled-down silicon chips.

Additional advances in three-dimensional (3D) chips and DNA computing are on the horizon. While chips traditionally contain a single, flat layer of transistors, 3D chips can vertically stack multiple layers of transistors.

Connections within a chip are in essence shorter than connections between chips, such as a processor chip connected to memory chips, which today exist separately. With this stacked organization, data needn't travel so far to execute a computation – and this massively increases processing speed.

Although still in its early stages, DNA computing could transform the future of computers.

The great benefit of DNA is its staggering memory capacity, in that one cubic centimeter of DNA could store more information than one trillion music CDs!

We've already witnessed some of what's possible with DNA computing. In 2002, Israeli scientist Ehud Shapiro and his team developed a DNA-based computer that could perform 330 trillion operations per second – more than 100,000 times the speed of the fastest PC at that time.

The Singularity Is Near Key Idea #3:

Over the next few decades, computers will learn to do everything humans can do, only better. Sure, computers can work quickly and efficiently, yet most of us wouldn't necessarily think of a computer as intelligent. A computer lacks insight, social intelligence and consciousness.

But this won't always be the case – and may change sooner than you think. Computer scientists today are exploring ways for computers to emulate what makes humans unique.

Let's take how the human brain works. Given sufficient scanning equipment, scientists may be able to accurately pinpoint exactly how the brain operates when you perform an "intelligent" act.

For instance, a scientist could track which neurons fire when you observe a person's facial expressions, or read a poem. These findings could then be translated into complex algorithms, or formulas that can be understood and processed by computers.

By 2030, these discoveries will give computer scientists the tools to reverse engineer the human brain. That is, they could build and program a computer that could imitate the human brain, and even become conscious – the advent of true artificial intelligence.

So what other changes are ahead? Certainly the computational power of artificial intelligence will exceed the capacity required to emulate all the functions of the human brain.

Scientists predict that it'll take between 100 trillion (ten to the power of 14) and ten quadrillion (ten to the power of 16) calculations per second (CPS) to do so.

How did scientists reach this figure? They measured how many CPS it took to simulate specific brain functions, such as the localization of sound, and what percent of the brain was involved in performing such a task. Then they extrapolated the results to make predictions about the rest of the brain.

In the future, it might not be unusual for your smartphone to be smarter than you are today!

But it's not just machines that will reap the benefits of such advances. The next book summary will explain that humans will benefit, too.

The Singularity Is Near Key Idea #4:

Nanobots will be the new doctors. Patrolling our insides, they'll cure illness and repair damage.

Over the centuries, the medical community has made significant breakthroughs in treating afflictions once thought incurable. Yet humans are still vulnerable to many deadly diseases and other maladies.

The good news is advances in robotics and nanotechnology over the next few decades will help people resist and even overcome physical afflictions.

How? Through the use of small, nanotechnological robots, called nanobots.

By putting these nanobots in your body, you will be able to alleviate any ailment or sickly bug that threatens your health. As nanobots can self-replicate, just one visit to the doctor's (for an initial nanobot injection) will be sufficient to keep you healthy for the long term.

But what will nanobots do exactly? These small fighters will be able to eliminate toxins, viral DNA and bacteria from your bloodstream. Just as our white blood cells fight pathogens in our bodies, nanobots will do the same, but will be far more effective in doing so.

Nanobots will also be able to clean plaque from blood vessels, the buildup of which poses a risk of heart disease or stroke, and could even cure Alzheimer's disease by eliminating dangerous chemical deposits in the brain.

These tiny robots could even be deployed to deliver medication to individual cells. For instance, a nanobot could deliver an aggressive cancer medication specifically to cancerous cells, thus keeping a patient from suffering common, systemic side effects such as nausea or hair loss.

It might even be possible to control your own nanobots via the internet.

Nanobots could also be used to repair damaged genes by scanning and monitoring a cell's nucleus and ensuring that everything was in order.

Consider the example of sunburn. If you suffered a serious burn at the beach, you wouldn't need to worry about the future threat of skin cancer, as your nanobots would repair the sun-damaged DNA in all your affected cells!

The Singularity Is Near Key Idea #5:

Genetic disease will be a thing of the past. Gene therapy to repair damage will become the norm. Even though gene therapies have been talked about for decades, we still tend to think of our DNA as a fixed foundation of who we are – something that can't change easily, or even at all.

But we're discovering that this isn't the case. Soon, gene therapy will become a commonplace intervention. One method would be using a simple virus to transfer genes into human cells.

When scientists want to replace a defective gene with a healthy one, there's always the problem of how to transfer DNA into a defective cell. But there could be a way around this, using a virus as a sort of "gene taxi."

Many viruses are effective at delivering genetic material to human cells, so all that needs to happen is to exchange the genes the virus would deliver with therapeutic ones. For example, one research team in Glasgow used a modified virus to switch genes in a patient's blood vessels.

Gene therapy may also help to heal many acute illnesses with a straight-forward injection.

Different genes in people can elevate the risk for particular illnesses, such as diabetes. This doesn't mean that everyone with a particular gene will get the disease, but if you do have the gene, you'll need to be wary, managing your diet and keeping physically fit.

Other severe illnesses can be caused by a damaged or altered gene, as is the case with cancer or sickle-cell anemia.

The good news is, once gene therapies are in play, a virus can be injected into your bloodstream to "infect" your cells with therapeutic DNA. Then, once nanobots are able to watch over your health, it will become even easier to repair damaged DNA as soon as it's necessary.

The Singularity Is Near Key Idea #6:

No more donor organs and risky surgery. In the future, we'll grow our own, from our own cells. Every day in the United States alone, 21 people die because of a lack of available donor organs.

In the near future, this will fortunately no longer be the case. We'll be able to clone the organs we need to save lives. Therapeutic cloning has the potential to vastly improve transplantation medicine.

Traditional organ transplant procedures have serious flaws. Usually, transplanted tissues come from an unrelated donor, a situation that often triggers the host's immune system to defend itself and potentially reject the transplanted organ.

To make sure a donor organ survives, the host's immune system must be suppressed at considerable cost, as impairing an immune system escalates the risk of contracting infectious disease or certain cancers.

An ideal transplant could be created using a host's own cells – and amazingly, we're already extremely close to doing just this.

Advances in biotechnology are offering ways to convert one type of cell, such as a skin cell, into another type, such as a pancreatic cell or nerve cell. Soon it will be possible to use these cells to grow custom-made organs in vitro.

But even if you don't require a transplant, cloning can provide a great way to revitalize the body in a non-invasive way. Once in the bloodstream, newly cloned cells can find their way to the appropriate organ or tissue, and set to work on replacing aging cells.

Thus, bit by bit, we'll be able to renew our bodies without the need for surgery. This is particularly valuable when it comes to organs like the heart, because as we age, our bodies become unable to replace older heart cells quickly enough.

So nanotechnology and cloning will help us sustain and renew our bodies, yet here we're still talking about a biological human body. These "old-school" bodies are quite different from the radically new types of bodies we'll begin to inhabit in the 2030s and 2040s.

The Singularity Is Near Key Idea #7:

Ready to become a bionic man or woman? Or perhaps something in between? The choice is yours. Retinal implants. Pacemakers. Cochlear implants. It may sound like the stuff of science fiction, but we're already on our way to becoming cyborgs.

Today plenty of people think nothing of hearing aids for the ear or lens implants for the eye. But these small adjustments are just the beginning. Around the year 2030, your body will be more non-biological than biological.

By this time, many of your organs will be replaced by electronic devices with the power to vastly enhance your body's performance.

Here's where nanobots come in again. Your heart, lungs and blood will be replaced by respirocytes, or nanobots that deliver oxygen to the bloodstream and remove carbon dioxide. Respirocytes will be so efficient that you could run an Olympic sprint for 15 minutes without taking a single breath!

Likewise, you won't need a digestive tract or kidneys, as you'll have feeding nanobots to deliver nutrients to every cell and elimination nanobots to clean up and leave the body, taking the waste with them. As a result, humans won't suffer from vitamin deficiency or be overweight.

As we push past the 2030s, our bodies will undergo a fundamental, liberating makeover.

We'll still preserve the body's functions as we know them, with nanobots interacting with biological cells. But by the late 2030s, we'll exchange this "body 2.0" with something far more durable and renewable, a "body 3.0."

This new body will be made up of "foglets," or nanobots that can assume any form and can directly manipulate visual information and sound waves, meaning you could create any projection you wish people to see or hear.

These foglets will give you the ability to change your appearance at will. If you wanted to, you could morph from Spock to a supermodel in a matter of seconds!

The Singularity Is Near Key Idea #8:

Artificial Intelligence and human intelligence will merge, and humans will become supersmart. As developments in brain-computer interfaces improve, the boundaries between artificial intelligence (AI) and human intelligence will begin to blur.

Whether you want to enhance your brain with a memory chip, plug into a Matrix-style simulated reality or steer a car using only your thoughts, you'll need a powerful brain-computer interface.

Scientific labs worldwide are already exploring new possibilities for brain-computer interfaces.

In 2003, German semiconductor maker Infineon, with assistance from the Max Planck Institute, created a "neurochip," or a chip that's directly connected to living nerve cells.

Using around 16,000 sensors, the chip can survey the electrical activity of several cells at once. With such chips, researchers can investigate how nerve tissues react to electrical stimulation, and thus discover more about the future possibilities of neuron-computer interaction.

Once these neurochip implants have made their way into our brains and our thoughts, it will be nearly impossible to distinguish between human intelligence and AI.

And with implants like these, we humans are going to become incredibly intelligent.

First we'll use memory chips to greatly expand our long-term memories, which means no more frustrating "tip-of-the-tongue" syndrome, as we'll be able to recall information at will.

Chips will expand our working memory capacity, which is strongly linked to intelligence. We'll be able to process data and make calculations far better than we've ever experienced.

By the end of the 2030s, your brain will also use nanobots to connect to the internet and download whatever information you want to know – just like Neo "knew" kung fu in The Matrix.

The Singularity Is Near Key Idea #9:

Around the year 2045, the world will change beyond recognition. The singularity will have arrived. The future we've talked about may seem weird or scary – but it's also amazing. Just think about all those nanobots coursing through your blood and brain! While not yet a reality, such concepts are still based in what we know and can comprehend.

Around 2045, however, the world will experience the "singularity." Then things will really get weird.

The singularity will be a fundamental shift in human history, a change beyond anything we can imagine today.

The developments we've seen so far will expand even further. In 2045, with just $1,000, you'll be able to purchase a computer a billion times more intelligent than all humanity combined.

Machines will be able to think and communicate so rapidly that humans won't be able to understand any of it. Machines too will develop revolutionary technologies in a matter of days.

In the future we'll be equipped to fight most illnesses; but by 2045, we'll have the means to become virtually immortal!

In the post-singularity world, intelligence will unfold throughout the universe.

Computer chips will eventually reach a physical limit. Once this limit has been reached, computers will have to increase in size to keep increasing in power, and they'll do this quickly.

Soon, more and more of the earth will be set up as a giant computer. This will likely involve the work of nanobots, turning objects into intelligent systems.

Nanobots require carbon, accessible through dead wood or ashes, for example, to self-replicate. The resultant group of nanobots will then organize themselves into a computer. Afterwards, even the materials of stars and planets will be reorganized to be transformed into computers!

The Singularity Is Near Key Idea #10:

A future run by sentient robots isn't perfect. Nanobots could malfunction, and cause havoc on earth.

Does the prospect of a singularity creep you out? Maybe even terrify you?

Well, the concept itself shouldn't. Thanks to your brain implants, by 2045 you'll be highly intelligent and have no problem keeping up with the rapidly evolving world.

Before then, however, something could go wrong. The most likely scenario involves nanobots and their ability to self-replicate.

Once nanobots are introduced into our bodies, we'll need lots of them to do the jobs we set for them. So it makes sense if nanobots can replicate themselves.

Nanobots assigned to your brain or immune system, for example, will need to be replaced as soon as possible if they're destroyed. If you lose too many, your body may simply stop functioning – just as if in a normal body, too many brain cells are destroyed.

So the most efficient way to replace nanobots is to have them self-replicate.

But this is not without consequence, as self-replicating nanobots could run amok.

Nanobots could be infected with a virus that turns them into destructive bots, tampering with their ability to self-regulate. A worst-case scenario would be if infected nanobots started acting like cancer cells, self-replicating without limit.

Out-of-control nanobots in the brain is no laughing matter. But if nanobots started to multiply outside a body, it could be as catastrophic as a nuclear explosion.

Carbon atoms are the building blocks of nanobots, and they require carbon to survive. Yet if nanobots were to replicate uncontrollably, they might decimate the earth's biomass, or material from living or dead plants, animals and humans.

It would take a mere 130 replications before all biomass – that is, all life on earth – would be destroyed. This would be quick, from between three hours and a few days!

Providing nanobots don't take over, humanity is in for a remarkable future.

Everyone who lives to see 2045 may "live" forever, transform into a powerful cyborg and communicate daily with supersmart, sentient robots.

Final summary The key message in this book:

Over the next few decades, artificial intelligence will eclipse biological human intelligence. But we will also become "artificially" intelligent. Gradually, our biological bodies and brains will be replaced and enhanced by devices, and humanity will be altered beyond anything we can imagine.

Suggested further reading: *The Second Machine Age* by Erik Brynjolfsson and Andrew McAfee

The Second Machine Age examines how technological progress is drastically changing our society, and why this development is not necessarily positive. It compares the rapid development of computer technology to the advent of the steam engine, which once catapulted the world into an Industrial Revolution.

VR NOTES 12

VR Related Films

The following films provide a glimpse, even if only partial, of the possibilities of virtual reality, especially if it is connected with sophisticated machine intelligence.

BRAINSTORM

LAWNMOWER MAN

INCEPTION

MINORITY REPORT

TOTAL RECALL

BLADE RUNNER

READY PLAYER ONE

TRON

VANILLA SKY

JOHNNY MNEMONIC

MATRIX

TRANSCENDENCE

FREE GUY

A.I. ARTIFICIAL INTELLIGENCE

Books on VR

Although this is by no means an exhaustive list, these are books that give a deeper and richer understanding of all things digitally related, particularly in connection with A.I. and Virtual Reality.

DAWN OF THE NEW EVERYTHING | *Jaron Lanier*

THE SINGULARITY IS NEAR | *Ray Kurzweil*

LIFE 3.0 | *Max Tegmark*

INEVITABLE | *Kevin Kelly*

READY PLAYER ONE | *Ernst Cline*

THE HISTORY OF THE FUTURE | *Blake J. Harris*

REALITY+ | *David Chalmers*

INFINITE REALITY | *Jim Blascovich, Jeremy Bailenson*

ON THE FUTURE | *Martin Rees*

THE ALIGNMENT PROBLEM | *Brian Christian*

VIRTUAL REALITY | *Samuel Greengard*

THE SIMULATION HYPOTHESIS | *Rizwan Virk*

THE VIRTUAL PHILOSOPHERS | Russell Savage

FUTURE PRESENCE | *Peter Rubin*

VR Timeline

GlobalData Technology

The history of virtual reality (VR) is longer than you might think. VR is entering its second generation, which is expected to have greater appeal to consumers as well as enterprises compared to the previous generation. VR technology has evolved significantly over the past five years, with improvements on both the hardware and software side. However, issues such as latency, nausea, high prices, and underdeveloped ecosystems have been obstacles to widespread adoption. VR companies are increasingly using AI and cloud technologies to develop stronger ecosystems, while the arrival of 5G promises to address the latency and nausea issues.

Invented in the 1950s, VR's development has experienced peaks and troughs. The first VR head-mounted display (HMD) system, The Sword of Damocles, was invented in 1968 by computer scientist Ivan Sutherland and his student Bob Sproull. Meanwhile, the term "virtual reality" was popularised by Jaron Lanier in the 1980s. Ten years later, VR was used for training and simulation in the US military and the National Aeronautics and Space Administration (NASA). Mass production of VR systems began in the early 1990s, led by Virtuality, which opened dedicated VR arcades. Contemporary VR devices emerged with the introduction of the PC-connected Oculus Rift prototype in 2010. Between 2014 and 2017, the market progressed from PC-tethered headsets (e.g. the HTC Vive) to console-tethered headsets (e.g. Sony's PSVR) and mobile-tethered headsets (e.g. Samsung GearVR and Google Cardboard). Untethered headsets (e.g. Oculus Go, Lenovo Mirage Solo, and HTC Vive Focus) arrived in 2018, making VR an independent platform.

The major milestones in the journey of the VR theme are set out in the timeline below.

THE HISTORY OF VIRTUAL REALITY

From Sensorama to Oculus Quest and beyond

1956 – Sensorama, considered to be one of the earliest VR systems, was invented.

1968 – The first VR HMD, The Sword of Damocles, was created.

1977 – Developed at MIT, the Aspen Movie Map enabled users to vitake a virtual tour of Aspen, Colorado.

1984 – Jaron Lanier founded VPL Research, one of the first companies to develop and sell VR products.

1991 – The first VR arcade machine, Virtuality, was introduced.

1994 – Sega introduced its VR-1 motion simulator in its SegaWorld arcades.

2007 – Google introduced Street View, which provides panoramic views of locations.

2010 – The first prototype of the Oculus Rift headset was designed.

2014 – Facebook acquired Oculus for $2bn.

2014 – Sony announced the launch of Project Morpheus, a VR headset for its PS4 console.

2015 – Apple awarded the patent for a head-mounted display apparatus.

2015 – Google launched Cardboard, which uses a head mount to turn a smartphone into a VR device.

2015 – Samsung launched the Gear VR headset.

2015 – The HTC Vive headset, developed by HTC and Valve, was unveiled at Mobile World Congress.

2016 – The first generation Oculus Rift device was released.

2016 – Sony's introduced PlayStation VR (PSVR).

2017 – Microsoft launched the Xbox One X, its VR-ready games console and headset.

2018 – Facebook revealed camera-loaded glasses optimised for 'social VR'.

2018 – Facebook released its untethered Oculus Go headset.

2018 – Lenovo's Mirage Solo, the first headset running Google Daydream, became available.

2019 – Sony announced that it had sold more than four million PSVR headsets.

2019 – Oculus 1 headset is released

2020 – Oculus 2 headset is released

2021 – More than 85 million VR headsets will be in use in China, according to PwC.

2022 – Oculus Pro/Cambria will be released

2023 – Cloud-based VR gaming will be increasingly prominent, supported by 5G networks.

2030 – VR will be a $28bn market, according to GlobalData forecasts.

Source: *This is an edited extract from the Virtual Reality – Thematic Research report produced by GlobalData Thematic Research.*

www.ingramcontent.com/pod-product-compliance
Lightning Source LLC
Chambersburg PA
CBHW030012290326
41934CB00005B/310